CAREERS FOR

SHUTTER
BUGS

& Other Candid Types

VGM Careers for You Series

CAREERS FOR

SHUTTER BUGS

& Other Candid Types

CHERYL MCLEAN

SECOND EDITION

VGM Career Books

Chicago   New York   San Francisco   Lisbon   London   Madrid   Mexico City
Milan   New Delhi   San Juan   Seoul   Singapore   Sydney   Toronto

49672570

Library of Congress Cataloging-in-Publication Data

McLean, Cheryl, 1957–
    Careers for shutterbugs & other candid types / Cheryl McLean. — 2nd ed.
        p.   cm. — (VGM careers for you series)
        ISBN 0-07-139035-9 (pbk.)
        1. Photography—Vocational guidance.   I. Title: Careers for shutterbugs and
other candid types.   II. Author.   III. Title.   IV. Series.

    TR154 .M38   2002
    770'.23—dc21   2002069119

To my own budding photographer,
my daughter Cassidy

1 2 3 4 5 6 7 8 9 0   LBM/LBM   1 0 9 8 7 6 5 4 3 2

ISBN 0-07-139035-9

McGraw-Hill books are available at special quantity discounts to use as premiums and sales promotions, or for use in corporate training programs. For more information, please write to the Director of Special Sales, Professional Publishing, McGraw-Hill, Two Penn Plaza, New York, NY 10121-2298. Or contact your local bookstore.

This book is printed on acid-free paper.

Contents

Acknowledgments   vii

CHAPTER ONE   **The Changing Face of Photography**
Introduction to Photography Careers   1

CHAPTER TWO   **The Digital Revolution**
Computers and Their Impact on Photography   23

CHAPTER THREE   **The News Beat**
Photojournalism and Press Photography   41

CHAPTER FOUR   **Say Cheese**
Portrait and People Photography   69

CHAPTER FIVE   **The Selling Game**
Commercial and Advertising Photography   85

CHAPTER SIX   **The Independent Shutterbug**
Freelance Photography   99

CHAPTER SEVEN   **On the Road Again**
Travel Photography   129

CHAPTER EIGHT   **Natural Wonders**
Nature and Wildlife Photography   147

CHAPTER NINE **Serving the Public**
Government and Military Photography 157

CHAPTER TEN **The World at Work**
Corporate and Industrial Photography 171

CHAPTER ELEVEN **The Fantastic Voyage**
Scientific and Medical Photography 183

CHAPTER TWELVE **On Gallery Walls**
Fine Art Photography 195

CHAPTER THIRTEEN **More Careers for Shutterbugs**
Related Opportunities in Photography 207

About the Author 231

Acknowledgments

would like to thank the organizations and individuals for the tremendous help they gave in the preparation of this manuscript, both in its original form and in this second edition. You will find their names sprinkled throughout the text, offering their words of wisdom and the benefit of their experience. I met many of these people through America Online's Kodak Photography Forum and through Internet searches for people living interesting lives doing the work they love. I was delighted and surprised by the generosity of each one of them. It's not a cliché—I couldn't have done it without them!

Special appreciation goes to Micki Reaman, who helped update all of the specifics on books and periodicals and professional organizations. I also deeply appreciate the delightful working relationship I enjoy with my editors, Denise Betts and Katherine Hinkebein.

CHAPTER ONE

The Changing Face of Photography

Introduction to Photography Careers

There's an old adage that goes something like this: Picture takers are a dime a dozen, but a real photographer is golden. Anyone can take pictures. Even my mother manages to get our heads in the picture frame some of the time. The burgeoning popularity of digital cameras and 35 mm point-and-shoot cameras, with their sophisticated light metering and focusing, can give even the most indifferent picture taker a degree of success.

But a photographer produces much more than a snapshot, much more than a quick recording of an occasion when the family gathered around the Thanksgiving Day dinner or when the tour bus stopped at a particularly breathtaking vista. A photographer gives you the moment itself, captured in a way that fills in the sounds and smells and textures that stimulated the senses at the instant the photograph was taken. A photographer tells a story, makes you long to see that enchanting view for yourself, brings to life a fleeting image that most of the world might have missed had it not been for the photographer's keen eye and deft touch with a camera.

A photographer has a passion for the craft itself and thrills when a photograph achieves its potential. A real photographer has not necessarily published or shown work beyond an immediate circle of family and friends but has tremendous potential to turn those talents toward a profitable and enjoyable career.

1

This book is devoted to those photographers who have developed—or have a desire to develop—their abilities and a photographer's eye and who want to take that extra step toward using a passion for photography to make a living.

....

Photography's Beginnings

The word *photography* was first coined in 1839 by Sir John Herschel, who combined derivations of Greek words for *light* and *writing* to describe the writing with light created when silver salts darken upon exposure to light. But the concept of photography—fixing an image on an alternate surface—was first mentioned by a fifth-century Chinese philosopher named Mo-Ti. He created an inverted image on a wall by allowing light rays to pass through a pinhole into a dark room, a technique later defined as a camera obscura, Latin for dark room. Leonardo da Vinci in 1490 described a similar technique used as an aid to drawing. In 1558, Giovanni Battista della Porta recommended the addition of a convex lens to the camera opening, or aperture, to sharpen the image and a mirror to reflect the image to the drawing surface. Sixteenth-century Dutch scientist Reinerus Gemma-Frisius used a camera obscura for observing the solar eclipse in 1544.

The camera obscura eventually led to the development of a portable box camera, first used as a drawing tool in the seventeenth century and two hundred years later modified to contain a light-sensitive material to permanently record the image. Joseph Niépce used a material that hardened under exposure to light to produce the first successful photograph in 1826, an image that required an eight-hour exposure. His partner, Louis Daguerre, experimented further and in 1839 developed the daguerreotype, a means of developing photographic plates that drastically reduced the exposure time—only half an hour was required!

The daguerreotype brought photography to a larger audience and spurred investigation into less expensive materials for creating photographic images. An early rival to Daguerre, William

Henry Fox Talbot of England developed the Calotype in 1835, a paper negative that allowed multiple prints to be developed on paper. The quality was inferior, but the advantage was that an unlimited number of prints could be made much more cheaply than the cost of a single silver-plate daguerreotype.

In 1851, Frederick Scott Archer introduced collodion prints, a new process, that coated a glass plate with light-sensitized egg treated with potassium iodide and washed with an acid solution of silver nitrate. The detail created with this method was exceptional, but exposures were so slow that only architecture and landscapes were suitable subjects.

Portrait photography didn't experience a major advance until the development of dry-plate processes in the 1870s. Dr. Richard Maddox discovered that gelatin could be used instead of glass for the photographic plate. Then George Eastman introduced flexible film in 1884, building on the development of celluloid in the 1860s. In 1888, Eastman produced the box camera, opening new opportunities for future generations of photographers.

The Future of Photography

Photography today is experiencing a radical transformation on a massive scale and at an unprecedented pace as a result of the ongoing computer revolution. Digital imagery is considered by many to be still in its infancy—even though the developments have been staggering in recent years. Some futurists even predict that eventually film will become obsolete. Most, however, feel that, as with the "paperless society" predicted with the development of personal computers, the "filmless society" is equally unrealistic. When daguerreotypes first enjoyed popularity, some predicted it would mean the end of painting as an art form. In the end, painting flourished, although it was influenced tremendously by the advent of photography. In the current transition, digital photography, rather than replace its silver-based predecessor, will undoubtedly spur deeper exploration of film as an art form.

Digital photography began with the creation of digital backs that could be attached to conventional cameras that would record the image electronically. Digital photography allows for instant evaluation and decision making. No longer does the photographer need to wait for film to be processed and prints made before determining whether a photo shoot accomplished its goals.

The pace of change in this field is so swift that the only sure bet is that you will find a whole new array of products and technologies on the market by the time this book hits the shelves. Chapter 2 discusses the digital revolution and the impact changes in technology have had on various photography careers.

Careers for Shutterbugs

Most professional photographers choose to specialize according to their particular interests. This book covers a wide range of career options, including advertising, industrial, portrait, wedding, nature, and fine art photography. For those more interested in the technical rather than creative aspects of photography, careers in science and medical photography, processing and printing, and repair and servicing are also discussed.

For the generalist and independently minded photographer, a career as a freelancer might be the perfect choice. Of the more than 131,000 professional full-time photographers in the nation in 2000, more than half were self-employed, which is an unusually high percentage. This includes the numerous photographer-owned portrait and commercial studios, as well as freelance photographers who contract with magazines or advertising agencies.

Where the Jobs Are

According to the *Occupational Outlook Handbook,* most employed photographers, those working for a regular salary, can be found in portrait or commercial studios. Most others were employed with newspapers, magazines, advertising agencies, television studios, and government agencies. Their titles might be photo editor, staff photographer, assistant photographer, or chief photographer. The highest concentration of photography professionals per capita is in major metropolitan areas.

Future Prospects

The job outlook in photography, according to the *Occupational Outlook Handbook,* is encouraging. Employment in photography is expected to increase as fast as the average for all occupations through 2010 and faster than average in some sectors. Demand for portrait photographers should increase along with population growth, and with the expansion of electronic publishing, photographers who can provide digital images for E-zines, as they're commonly called, will be needed. Some decline in small-business commercial photography may be seen as the ease and accessibility of digital photography expands and some companies begin taking their own photographs. High-quality images produced by trained professionals will always be the standard for commercial and advertising photography, however.

Keen competition in virtually every area of photography means that you will need strong technical skills and creativity along with an ability to represent yourself well to prospective employers or clients. In this field, as in many others, however, persistence and patience are the keys to success, as well as an ability to adapt to rapidly changing technology. Photographers who hope to succeed as freelancers need business skills as well—the ability to write business plans, prepare bids, write contracts, hire models and assistants, obtain necessary permissions, secure copyright protection, and maintain financial records.

Income Potential

The range of earnings for photographers varies considerably and depends to a large degree on both the type of photography and the amount of time spent developing your career or client base. According to the *Occupational Outlook Handbook,* the median annual earnings for salaried photographers was $22,300 in 2000. The top 10 percent earned more than $46,890, and the lowest 10 percent earned less than $13,760. Salary levels for specific photography specialties are discussed in subsequent chapters.

For many photographers, the question of income is secondary to the many other benefits of a career in photography. The autonomy, the creative potential, and, for many, the freedom to choose one's own hours can mean more than high earning potential.

Education and Training

The technical expertise and creative eye required for a successful photography career can be gained by following a number of paths. No method offers a surefire first step into your new career, but some general advice applies to most areas of photography. The following is a list of abilities students develop through a program of photography study at a community college in Washington. The list of program goals provides a good outline for the skills and knowledge you want to develop as you learn your craft. Before embarking on their careers, graduates of the program would be able to:

- Understand and use design elements and technical skill to create effective visual images
- Understand and use a variety of still, video, television, and digital camera equipment, including small-, medium-, and large-format cameras
- Develop black-and-white photographs using a variety of basic, advanced, and special techniques
- Use computer equipment and software to create, use, scan, and manipulate photographic images for use in printed materials as well as in video and multimedia productions

- Demonstrate knowledge of values associated with commercial, documentary, journalistic, and artistic photography

Start in High School

If you're still in high school, get involved with the yearbook, student newspaper, and any other school publications that require the services of photographers. You might be rewarded with academic credit or perhaps even a supply of film or a modest payment, but the true reward is the experience you gain working for a publication and seeing your photographs in print.

Classes in photography can be extremely valuable, particularly those giving you experience in operating your camera, processing and developing film, working with photo-editing software, and taking photographs in a variety of situations. Get as much experience doing your own darkroom work—including the digital darkroom—as possible because this provides tremendous insight into what happens to the film once it leaves the camera and what you can do before you shoot to influence the end result.

And given the rapid progression toward a digital environment in many photography careers, courses or workshops in digital photography and computer applications such as Adobe Photoshop will be increasingly important. You can find online seminars through the websites of various software companies and professional associations, and most community colleges offer a variety of workshops and seminars for both beginning and advanced students.

College Opportunities

In college, sign on with the yearbook or newspaper staff. Make yourself known to the art director in the publications office or the editor of the alumni magazine or newspaper. The more experience you gain, the more material you have to choose from when preparing your first portfolio.

Virtually every college, university, and vocational-technical college in the country offers photography courses, and several offer bachelor of fine arts degrees, which indicates a degree of commitment to the creative use of photography. Photojournalism is another major area of study at many colleges. These courses are usually offered within the journalism school or department.

Some of the areas of study available in colleges offering two-year associate's degrees (associate of arts and sciences or A.A.S.), four-year bachelor's degrees (bachelor of arts, bachelor of fine arts, or bachelor of science), and graduate degrees (master of arts, master of fine arts, or master of science) include the following:

- Advertising photography
- Aerial photography
- Airbrushing and retouching
- Animation
- Archaeological photography
- Architectural photography
- Audiovisual production
- Biomedical photography
- Botanical photography
- Color photography and printing
- Computer animation
- Corporate photography
- Digital image construction
- Digital photography
- Documentary photography
- Editorial photography
- Electronic field production
- Electronic still photography
- Fashion photography
- Fine art photography
- Food photography
- Forensic photography
- High-speed photography

- History of photography
- Illustration photography
- Imaging and photographic technology
- Industrial photography
- Medical and dental photography
- Nature photography
- Optical photography
- Photography for publication
- Portfolio production
- Science photography
- Sports photography
- Studio photography
- Studio video production
- Videography
- Visual journalism/communication

A college degree is not, however, a prerequisite to a successful photography career. One photojournalist I spoke with advises would-be press photographers to major in anything but photography. He asserts that photography as a craft can be learned on one's own or on the job and that the broader educational background of a degree in liberal arts or other disciplines enhances your ability to understand and interpret the world around you and thus makes you a better photographer.

Photography Courses and Workshops

Nevertheless, basic courses in photography can be an extremely efficient means of developing the technical skills you need. These courses generally instruct students about how to use the equipment—camera, lenses, light meters, lighting—as well as how to develop and print photographs.

Many professional photographers caution against courses that try to teach a particular style or approach to photography. This, they suggest, is something you develop over the years as you take photographs, evaluate them, and learn from them.

Workshops in specific genres of photography can, however, provide an opportunity to work closely with a master photographer and profit from the feedback of others. There are workshops for amateurs and professionals, covering everything from infrared landscape photography to studio lighting techniques.

Major camera and film manufacturers often hold workshops or seminars for professionals on new products and their uses that can help you keep up-to-date on technical innovations in photography. *Photographer's Market* includes a listing of some 140 workshops in its annual publication. Photography workshops are also listed in *Guide to Photography Workshops* and *Photographer's Forum: Photography and Travel Workshop Directory*. Professional associations also offer workshops for members on a wide range of subjects. A free online directory of more than two thousand photography, film, and new media workshops worldwide can be found at http://photoworkshops.shawguides.com.

Continuing Education

Even professional photographers can benefit from additional training or expanded opportunities for gaining experience. Those on the leading edge of publications and communications technology caution photographers that if they want to hold a place in the future, they will need to become familiar with the new world of digital photography. Courses or seminars in the new technology are offered by computer software companies, computer manufacturers, and the makers of the new digital cameras, as well as those colleges or universities with the budgets to afford expensive equipment. Chapter 2 covers this subject in more detail.

A Program of Self-Study

Becoming a photographer involves, above all, taking a lot of photographs. Whether this is part of a prescribed curriculum or on your own, you need to develop technical proficiency and a thorough knowledge of your equipment and its potential and limitations, and you need to develop your photographer's eye.

Go on self-assignments. Give yourself a task to accomplish or a visual problem to solve, then use your camera to fulfill the assignment. As you take photographs, keep a notebook of the lighting conditions, the meter readings, the aperture and shutter speed settings. Photograph the same subject, altering one or more of the variables. Take more notes. When you process and print your film, take notes for the darkroom phase of the process.

Then study the photographs. Evaluate them for technical quality—contrast, sharpness of focus, depth of field. Evaluate them for aesthetic quality—composition, lighting, texture, content, or message. What worked well? What didn't work? What could you do to improve the photograph? Take more photographs, more notes, and evaluate again.

Meanwhile, read whatever you can get your hands on. Look at photographs by photographers you admire as well as those whose work leaves you cold. Ask yourself why you like one photograph but don't like another. Gather as much of a sense of the history and development of photography as you can. Join a photography club to find others who can help provide insight and feedback about your work.

In the long run, though, the number and type of courses you've taken won't be what will get you the job or the assignment. That requires great photos. And you only get those by shooting roll after roll after roll of film and becoming your own best critic. Ernest Hemingway once said that to be a writer you need to have "a built-in, shock-proof crap detector." The same is true in photography or any creative field. You need to know when your work is good—and when it's not! Then work hard to bring your photographs to their full potential.

Equipment and Darkroom

If you haven't already invested heavily in equipment and darkroom setups, you might want to move slowly in this direction. Tim Mirren, a commercial photographer with a thriving freelance business, started out with only one 35 mm camera body and two lenses. He took his black-and-white film to the darkroom at a community arts center, which he joined for $25 per year plus a usage fee for the chemicals. Color film he sent to a custom lab for processing. As he got assignments, he took half the payment to live on and he poured the other half into additional equipment. Over time, he acquired three 35 mm cameras, a medium-format camera, and a four-by-five-inch camera for studio work, as well as lighting equipment, a private darkroom, and a studio facility.

"That way I was able to build my commitment to this career as I built my experience base," Tim explains. "I didn't have to go into debt and then hope the jobs would come."

Most photographers, whether on staff or independent, prefer to use their own cameras, with the exception of portrait studios or large corporate situations requiring special, highly expensive equipment. The equipment you need depends on the type of photography you'll be doing. Studio portrait photographers most likely work with medium- or large-format cameras. Wedding photographers, who shoot both portraits after the ceremony and event photographs during the ceremony, often use both 35 mm and four-by-five cameras, as well as video cameras and digitals. Unless it's an extremely high-end piece of equipment, most digital cameras have a delayed response to allow the lens to focus after the shutter is pressed. Such a delay can wreak havoc when trying to capture particular moments, such as the bride's throwing the bouquet or cutting the wedding cake.

Photojournalists, nature and wildlife photographers, and others who must be able to move quickly on the job most likely use 35 mm cameras or high-end digital cameras and have more than one camera body, each loaded with a different type of film or lens. Their work often requires a quick response, and they don't have time to change film or lenses to get the best shot. Professionals working with big-budget news media often use high-end—and therefore extremely high-priced—digital cameras that have no shutter delay and can shoot several frames in a second.

Tim cautions that photographers embarking on a career should wait to buy the best rather than buy several lenses of lesser quality just to fill the camera bag. As a professional, you'll need your equipment to function at an optimal level. The same is true, he says, for a darkroom.

"I didn't invest in my own darkroom for a long time because I had access to one so inexpensively, and for color work I could always build processing expenses into the job," Tim says. "I set up the darkroom mostly for my own enjoyment. There are very acceptable alternatives available for getting professional processing and printing."

Getting Started

Like educational background, your first steps into your career will vary according to your interests and the opportunities in your area. Each chapter offers specific advice for that career path, but some advice is general enough to apply to whichever field you choose. Before you approach your first job interview or presentation to a prospective client, you need to have demonstrated your technical expertise, your aesthetic or creative ability, and your previous experience. The tools for demonstrating these accomplishments are the portfolio and the resume.

The Photographer's Portfolio

Whether you're hoping to land an assignment with the local newspaper or a full-time job with a New York advertising agency, as a photographer you need a portfolio. The portfolio is a collection of your work that shows what you are capable of, what you have done, and what your work is like in terms of its approach or style.

"Your portfolio should include the best of what you've done," says Harrison Branch, professor of photography at Oregon State University. "You need to carefully evaluate each image, look at how it fits with others as part of a presentation, and then ask what the entire package says about you as a photographer."

It's not unusual to tailor separate portfolios for specific jobs, making sure each communicates something specific about you as a photographer. Chapters 7 and 12 provide more detail on how to develop strong portfolios.

The Resume

As a photographer, your resume is often what gets you in the door to show your portfolio. Your resume alone won't get you a job—that's up to your photographs. But it can get you interviewed, and that's an important enough step to warrant spending time polishing your resume.

For the most part, resumes should fit on a single sheet of paper. If you have long lists of exhibitions or publications to your credit, you might add a line at the bottom that in addition to a portfolio, you have both references and an exhibit or publication list available on request. Then make sure you have these lists ready if they are requested.

The resume needs to include all relevant education and training, work experiences, military service, or specialized skills that will make it clear you have the credentials needed to get the job done. Professional memberships and other activities that relate to your career field are also important to include.

Several books are available on how to prepare a job-winning resume. You might also want to consult someone who specializes in resumes or another professional in the field before you consider it finished.

Competitions

Photography contests are being held almost constantly, and they provide both amateurs and professionals an opportunity to gain recognition, remuneration, and publication. Two newsletters, *Entry* and *Photographic Resource Newsletter,* provide regular listings of photographic competitions and juried exhibitions.

Professional and amateur-oriented photography magazines frequently hold their own competitions, as well as publish listings of other requests for contest-entry submissions. *Petersen's Photographic Magazine,* for example, sponsors monthly contests and publishes the winning photographs in subsequent issues. Kodak, Fuji, Nikon, Minolta, Olympus, and other film and camera manufacturers open annual photography competitions and use the winning photographs in advertising campaigns and other promotional publications.

In addition to established competitions, watch for photo contests offered by your local newspaper or chamber of commerce. Consider them photography assignments, then go out and take photographs with an eye toward winning first prize. Not only will this give you additional experience with photographing, it will provide insight into what it means to work "on assignment," with a specific task to complete or problem to solve. If you win, of course you receive both the prize and a "tear sheet," or page torn from the magazine, for your portfolio, as well as an impressive line on your resume. Competitions sometimes have themes, but general competitions are open to all photographers, who then select a category of competition to enter:

- Documentary
- Fashion illustration
- Feature
- Food illustration
- General news event
- Personal vision or fine arts
- Pictorial or scenic
- Picture story or photo essay
- Portrait
- Sports
- Spot news
- Wildlife or nature

Some competitions require payment of an entry fee, which some photographers liken to buying a lottery ticket. The only other word of caution is to avoid contests that retain all rights to your prize-winning photographs. For a more detailed discussion of copyrights and rights sales, see Chapter 6.

Developing Your Job Prospects

Armed with a portfolio, a resume, and good portions of talent, determination, and patience, you're ready to plan your strategy. As you prepared your portfolio, you determined the kind of work you are seeking to do as a photographer.

Set some goals for the kind of job or the kind of employer you want to find. List all the things you have to offer in that situation. Then develop a list of prospective employers or clients who fit those requirements. Don't worry if they're not actively advertising for a photographer. Often, jobs are filled or assignments are given through the grapevine or because a persistent photographer kept in touch with an editor who expressed an interest.

If the kind of job you really want is out of reach for your experience or background, look for a job that's both related and that gives you an opportunity to add to your skills or knowledge base. Working in a camera store or processing lab gets you in contact with photographers and others in the business who can be a tremendous resource.

When you make job contacts, by phone or by cover letter, always ask for an opportunity to show your portfolio. Remember, it's your photographs that will get you hired. Regardless of the outcome of the portfolio presentation, be sure to follow through with a note of thanks. Call back if you haven't heard anything for a week or so after the presentation. Be sure the employer knows you're interested.

Internships

Working for a school publication provides a brief introduction to the work of photography, but it's vastly different from the real world of a daily newspaper or an advertising agency. An internship or apprenticeship in such an organization can give you a clearer sense of the demands and rewards offered in the various career paths in photography.

Many photojournalism programs at colleges and universities offer formal arrangements for internships with newspapers or magazines. In addition to the experience you gain, at the end of the internship, you've added a valuable line to your resume.

It is also possible to arrange for internships or apprenticeships on your own, although this involves almost as much perseverance as your ultimate job search. There are a number of avenues to follow, depending on the area of photography you wish to pursue. An aspiring photojournalist might ask to tag along with the photographer of a local daily or hang out in the darkroom and at the editorial desk with the photo editor for a few days.

Someone seeking a career in commercial or advertising photography might approach a studio owner with an offer of free or reduced-wage assistance in exchange for the opportunity to learn the ropes from a pro. Go in as if you were applying for the job of a lifetime, and be prepared for rejection. Cheap labor isn't necessarily always a bargain. It takes time to work with a novice, and a busy professional may not have time to spend training someone who doesn't have a demonstrated ability on which to build.

Assisting

Okay, you've graduated from college, you've prepared a dynamite portfolio of self-assignment photographs, you've maybe even spent a few weeks working side by side with a master photographer. You're ready to become a professional photographer, ready to take on the big-time jobs, right? Well, maybe. Photography is a highly competitive pursuit, and sometimes you need to be prepared to wade in shallower waters before you dive into the deep end.

Working as a photographer's assistant is an opportunity for you to gain what you need in order to swim with the big fish: experience. Regardless of the level of education you've received and the sophistication of your training, you still need experience to get the attention of top employers and clients.

As an assistant, you usually don't get to work behind the camera, but you do gain experience with everything else. You watch to see how the professional handles difficult lighting situations, unusual creative problems, or picky clients. The procedures for setting up a still life, making arrangements for a location shoot, working with models, and turning in film become commonplace.

Then when you've worked hard, shown talent, and proven your abilities, the photographer you work for won't have any qualms about recommending you when a job comes along that's too small or doesn't pay enough to cover high-priced professional rates. That's when you start to get experience behind the camera as well as behind the scenes.

Professional Associations

For every specialty in photography, there's a membership organization to provide information, networking, and support. Many of these offer student membership rates, and most publish regular newsletters or journals that provide a wealth of information. Employment listings are often included in that information.

Many seminars offer critique services, where experienced professionals review your photographs and provide feedback and advice on how to improve your work. This is an extremely valuable service for someone beginning a photography career.

Conventions, seminars, trade shows, and equipment purchase discounts are some of the extra benefits of membership. In addition, many offer group insurance plans for personal health and disability insurance for photographers working independently.

For someone seriously interested in pursuing a career in photography, membership in a professional organization is well worth the annual dues. Individual organizations are listed at the end of this and other chapters. Some of the more general membership associations include the American Society of Media Photographers, American Society of Picture Professionals, Pictorial Photographers of America, Professional Photographers of America, and Professional Women Photographers.

Online Resources

The Internet provides an amazing resource for information and support. You can research and buy equipment, hunt for jobs, and seek advice from other photographers in various online forums. Professional membership organizations have online sites where members may pose general questions or post notices about new developments in the field, issues of interest, and even job listings. Many organizations operate job information banks available to members only.

Keys to Success

Because photography has so much to offer as a career choice—and because taking photographs, seeing them in print, and then getting paid for it is just plain fun—there are a lot of people out there who'd like to do this for a living. Photography is a competitive field. To assure success, you need more than a camera and know-how. As you develop your skills, hone your talent, and add to your base of experience, remember to work on these fundamentals:

- Technical mastery
- A photographer's eye
- Business and marketing skills
- Determination
- Commitment
- Patience

The rewards are there if you're willing to go after them and work toward your goals. The following chapters outline some of the many choices you have as a photographer embarking on a career with your camera. Undoubtedly some career possibilities have been missed, but this book provides a sense of the broad range of possibilities and how you might begin to use your camera to turn something you love to do into what you do for a living.

....

For More Information

Organizations
American Society of Picture Professionals
409 South Washington Street
Alexandria, VA 22134
www.aspp.com

Canadian Association of Photographers & Illustrators in
  Communications (CAPIC)
100 Broadview Avenue, Number 322
Toronto, ON M4M 2E8
Canada
www.capic.org

Graphic Artists Guild
90 John Street, Suite 403
New York, NY 10038
www.gag.org

Women in Photography International
569 North Rossmore Avenue, Suite 604
Los Angeles, CA 90004
www.WomeninPhotography.org

Periodicals
Camera Arts
P.O. Box 2328
Corrales, NM 87048
www.cameraarts.com
>   (*Bimonthly magazine dedicated to the art and craft of small and
>   medium format photography.*)

Petersen's Photographic Magazine
6420 Wilshire Boulevard
Los Angeles, CA 90048
www.photographic.com
   (Monthly for amateur and semiprofessional photographers.)

Photo Techniques
6600 West Touhy Avenue
Niles, IL 60714
www.phototechmag.com
   (Bimonthly magazine for professionals covering darkroom technology and black-and-white, color, and digital photography.)

Popular Photography
Hacette Filipacchi Magazines Incorporated
1633 Broadway
New York, NY 10019
www.popphoto.com
   (Monthly magazine for amateur photographers. Website forum links with discussions of equipment, technique, and digital photography.)

Professional Photographer
Professional Photographers of America
229 Peachtree Street NE, Suite 2200
Atlanta, GA 30303
www.ppmag.com
   (Monthly magazine for members of PPA emphasizing technique and equipment for professionals.)

Shutterbug
5211 South Washington Avenue
Titusville, FL 32780
www.shutterbug.net
   (Monthly magazine of photography news, photo features, and equipment reviews.)

View Camera Magazine
P.O. Box 2328
Corrales, NM 87048
www.viewcamera.com
   (Bimonthly magazine dedicated to the art and craft of large-format photography.)

Books

Choosing a Career as a Professional Photographer, by Greg Roza.
Rosen Publishing Group, Incorporated.
Opportunities in Photography Careers, by Bervin Johnson.
McGraw-Hill/Contemporary.
Photographer's Market: 2,000 Places to Sell Your Photographs.
Writer's Digest.
The Law (in Plain English) for Photographers, by Leonard D.
Duboff. Allworth Press.

Online Resources

Apogee Photo Magazine, the oldest online magazine in the United
States, is devoted to all levels of photography expertise:
www.apogeephoto.com.
BetterPhoto.com is an online photography guide for amateur
photographers.
FotoInfo provides technical information on different aspects of
photography ranging from the chemistry behind developing
to general photography facts: www.fotoinfo.com.

CHAPTER TWO

The Digital Revolution

Computers and Their Impact on Photography

E very aspect of photography has been or will be affected by the development of computer and digital technology. The change has been dramatic, wide-reaching, and so rapid that it's nearly impossible to keep up with new developments.

Ray DeMoulin, former Kodak vice president and director of the Center for Creative Imaging, predicted in 1994, "Within five years most photographers will have used the computer to improve or modify their pictures in some way." That prediction has definitely come true and has been surpassed. It would be safe to say that most professional photographers have incorporated the digital world in some way into their regular working routines—whether through film or slide scanners for input to the computer, compact discs for saving images electronically, or digital cameras or digital camera backs for instant electronic image development.

At the 2002 Winter Olympics, for example, a majority of the professional photographers were shooting digitally. "With their deadlines, it's much faster and easier to edit and transmit digital images than it is to develop film and scan it," says Scott Frier, a Nikon professional markets representative who observed that 90 to 95 percent of the photographers using Nikon's Olympic Depot were using digital cameras. "But shooting digitally also saves a huge amount of money photographers would ordinarily spend on film and processing."

New developments in hybrid cameras may help photographers bring the best of both worlds to their work. Some of the latest possibilities are still in the development stage and many are still beyond the budgets of most photographers:

- a digital camera that prints on Polaroid film
- a film-based camera with an LCD preview that allows you to review images and dispose of those you don't like before burning them on the film
- a 35 mm camera containing both film and digital capability that allows switching quickly from one to the other
- a new silicon film that works with an adapter in a standard 35 mm camera, turning it into a digital camera
- a film-based camera that, when the film is processed, creates a digital copy of the photograph

Anyone contemplating a career in photography, at whatever level, must become well-versed in the new media. Even if you continue to use a traditional camera for taking your photographs, at some point in the process from shutter to print, the computer will enter the picture.

Digital technology is the wave of the future. Even the most reluctant old-school photographers are beginning to appreciate digital photography for what it is—just another tool, a different kind of oar with which to paddle the same boat. It's not the only future, and the wave may not have crested yet, but the whole world is riding it, and if you're not in there swimming, you could just get lost in the flotsam.

Digital Careers

Income opportunities in this field are high because of the demand and the level of expertise required. That may change as more and more people develop computer skills, but the photographer's eye will be valuable in the world of professional image making.

From the business side to the creative, computers continue to revolutionize the way photographers and others in the $225 billion infoimagery industry do business. Those who have embraced the technology are finding new opportunities and limitless possibilities for developing their own creativity. Although it's intimidating at first, and there's a steep learning curve, the new technology can ultimately mean an amazing amount of control and freedom for photographers.

Some photographers have embraced the technology because they are eager to try something new. Others see the benefits for the workplace in terms of cost and time savings. Still others look at the creativity that's possible in the digital darkroom.

Jeff Schewe, a professional advertising photographer based in Chicago, works in a photo-realist and photo-surrealist manner. He has found that electronic image editing makes producing his images a lot more workable. "Computer imaging has made the photography part of my life much simpler and easier, and the photography part has made computer imaging much simpler and easier," he told Apple Computer in an online forum about Adobe Photoshop. "I used to have to do extensive film testing and used all kinds of color correction filters just to get the film to look exactly the way I wanted, so I could have ultimate control. Now I don't have to worry about that. I just photograph the essence of what I need and then I manipulate and alter it in Photoshop."

What the Technology Means

Put simply, digital photography means that a photographic image is reduced, through the marvels of high mathematics and computer technology, to a set of digits or numeric codes, one for each pixel of space on the image. A pixel is a dot that forms an image when combined with a lot of other dots of varying hue, saturation, density, and brightness. The image on a television screen or computer screen is composed of pixels. In order to print or transmit an image, it must be broken into these dots.

The size of the dots determines the finished quality of the image. On a computer screen, the resolution is typically 72 dots, or pixels, per inch. New flat-screen monitors can have as many as 200 pixels per inch, which makes for a much sharper resolution. An image reproduced in a newspaper has much larger dots than one printed in a magazine on glossy paper. In printing technology, these dots are referred to as line screens. A newspaper reproduces images at a resolution (degree of sharpness) of 80 or 100 lines per inch (lpi). A magazine's photograph resolution is generally 133 or 150 lpi. A very high-quality printer of postcards or art prints might use a resolution as high as 175 or 200 lpi. For true photographic prints, the resolution pushes to 3750 or more lines.

All cameras—whether digital or traditional—respond to optical light waves. Traditional cameras use silver-based film that darkens when exposed to light. Digital cameras use light sensors that translate the light waves into electronic impulses that are in turn translated by a microprocessor into digital information. The digital information provides the numeric codes to define each pixel of the image as a specific color, hue saturation, brightness, and density. The more pixels the camera is capable of rendering, the more digital information is available and, therefore, the sharper and clearer the resulting photograph will be.

Technology Developments

It's virtually impossible for a book—with its long schedule of production and printing—to represent the "latest" developments in digital technology. As soon as I finish writing this sentence, there is sure to be another new product or software announced. Still, we can look at a snapshot of the world of technology and review the developments that have had the greatest impact on photography.

Photo CD, Picture CD, and DVD

Kodak's Photo CD has become a standard means of storing and viewing photographs originally produced with a traditional film camera. The Photo CD allows you to develop your 35 mm through four-by-five film, slides, or negatives onto compact discs that can be read by a CD-ROM drive attached to your computer or to your television set. Images are placed on the Photo CD at five different resolutions, from low-resolution suitable for on-screen viewing (128 x 192 pixels) to a high-resolution equivalent to printing an eight-by-ten photograph (2048 x 3072 pixels). A higher resolution (4096 x 6144) is available with Kodak Photo Pro CDs.

The Picture CD, a more recent development used primarily by everyday consumers rather than professional photographers, provides JPG-format images in one resolution (1024 x 1536), which is suitable for printing up to five-by-seven-inch prints on an ink-jet printer. JPG is a compressed file format that can be accessed from a wide variety of software programs. Picture CDs also come with both Macintosh and Windows software that allows you to view, store, and make minor edits in your photos.

Photo CDs look just like music CDs that have replaced record albums and cassette tapes as the medium for storing recorded music and the video DVDs that are rapidly replacing videocassettes. Both CDs and DVDs are digital media—the images and sounds are broken down into digital information that can be accessed randomly rather than in linear form, as with a video or cassette tape. DVD, which originally stood for digital video disc but now means digital versatile disc, was designed originally for video, audio, and multimedia. A single DVD has the capacity to store full-length feature films, high-quality digital audio in surround sound, and more than eight gigabytes of digital data.

Most new computers now come with the capability of creating—or burning—your own CDs. Some now have DVD-burning capability. DVD readers are capable of reading all CD formats, but eventually DVD will become the new standard.

The Digital Darkroom

In order to exploit the digital darkroom's capabilities, you will need a computer, monitor, CD-ROM drive, and the appropriate image-editing software. Photo CD images have been processed just as you would process your film, but often the image needs to be color corrected before it matches your intent. In the traditional darkroom, photographers often use filters and a variety of lenses and complete numerous tests when printing from film negatives. The process in the digital darkroom is remarkably similar. Adobe Photoshop has an even broader array of filters with which to adjust images, and the fine tuning that it's capable of has made a digital junkie of many a darkroom addict.

Be sure you have both the memory and hard disk storage capability to handle the large image files. Your computer's processor speed is also a factor in how efficiently you can work. A large, high-resolution color image can take up hundreds of megabytes of disk space, and you need to have at least as much RAM, or random-access memory, and twice as much available disk space in order to work with images in Photoshop. When setting up your digital darkroom, go for the fastest processor, the most memory, and the largest-capacity hard disk that you can afford. With the relentless advances in technology and software capability, it won't be long before you feel the need to upgrade.

Choosing a platform—Mac or PC—is perhaps less important than it once was. Previously, there was no comparison—the Macintosh was clearly more sophisticated when it came to digital imagery and graphics work. The gap has closed, but you'll find that most professionals are still using the Mac platform. "Most of the pro market uses Macs," explains Nikon's Scott Frier. "Professional photographers want the computer to do what they want to do. They're not computer people; they're photographers. They want the computer as a tool, not as an adventure. Also, the Mac has traditionally been the graphics machine, and things like iPhoto, ColorSync, and iDVD keep photographers loyal."

"Every Mac comes with a suite of free, elegant digital media programs, which are in most cases simpler and more capable than their Windows counterparts," according to Walter Mossberg, technology columnist for the *Wall Street Journal*. "There's iMovie, the easiest and best video editor I've seen. There's iTunes, a very nice MP3 music jukebox that can also burn audio CDs. There's iDVD, the best and simplest program I've tested for creating homemade

DVDs. And now, Apple has rounded out the quartet with iPhoto, a program for organizing, managing, and sharing digital photos." Although useful for professional photographers primarily for its organizational capabilities, iPhoto is great fun for novice users and provides connectivity to Photoshop for more serious image editing. It also coordinates with Apple's free web-page development software to incorporate photos on your own website.

Printing

To print your photographs from your digital darkroom, inexpensive ink-jet color printers can provide low-quality proofs for color photographs. But for not much more money, you can buy a high-end ink-jet with the capability of printing at near-photographic resolutions on specially coated papers. Large-format ink-jet printers—capable of printing twelve-by-nineteen-inch or more—with either four-color or six-color inks have become more affordable and will undoubtedly be even less expensive in coming years. Many fine art photographers use these large-format ink-jets and archival inks—which are designed to resist fading for at least a hundred years—for producing their final prints.

Color printers use the industry standard four-color ink process, and the computer translates the red-green-blue color mode into cyan-magenta-yellow-black color for printing. Dye-sublimation printers give very good reproduction for both color and black and white, but the cost of these printers means you'll most likely be taking your computer disc to a service bureau, unless you work for a large company that has its own high-resolution color printer.

Digital Cameras

When the first edition of the book was written, digital cameras were still in the new-technology phase. Quality was poor and prices were high. Today, even the least expensive digital camera produces images to equal the quality of their more-expensive predecessors. And the new digital cameras range from less than $50 for quick snapshot digitals to more than $20,000 for professional-quality studio models.

Digital photography began with the creation of digital backs that could be attached to conventional cameras that would record the image electronically. These were—and still are—used mostly by catalog and studio photographers. Among the first fully digital cameras were those developed primarily for photojournalists who need to capture images rapidly and get them to the newspaper in a hurry. The camera incorporated traditional camera lenses that enabled the photographer to work in much the same way as with traditional film-based photography.

The camera could be linked to a modem, which allowed images to be transmitted over normal phone lines to any computer or picture desk capable of receiving files in the specific digital format, or it could be hooked up directly to the computer and the images could be downloaded onto the computer's hard disk. The images could then be edited using image-editing software to prepare for insertion into the newspaper or news magazine.

Today, the functionality is essentially the same. The changes have come in terms of capacity, speed, connectivity, and quality. While early professional-level digital cameras could capture 1.3 megapixels of information, today such cameras are capable of 16 megapixels. And this is only the beginning.

A major new development—the Foveon X3 image sensor—is about to set off another new wave of technological advances. It is the first image sensor to capture red, green, and blue light at each and every pixel. Embedded in silicon and stacked in layers, three photodetectors for each pixel detect red, green, and blue light, which penetrate the silicon to different depths. All other sensors have thus far had only one detector per pixel. Each captured just one of the colors, and mosaic sensors filtered only 25 percent of the red and blue light and 50 percent of the green. The camera then had to interpolate the missed colors, which leads to some of the problems in digital image quality that traditional photographers are fond of pointing out. The first cameras to incorporate this technology are just now poising to enter the market and will undoubtedly be prohibitively expensive. However, as with all of the new technology, it won't be long before even newer developments drive the price down.

Cameras typically connect to the computer through a cable. Making sure your computer and camera can communicate is an important factor in deciding which camera to purchase. If you have an older computer that doesn't have USB or FireWire connection, your choice in digital cameras may be limited to something you can find used, unless you're ready to upgrade your computer system.

Scanning

Photographs can also be digitized on scanners that use light to "photograph" the photograph, film negative, slide, or transparency, and then translate the visual information into digital data. Scanning technology has been part of the traditional offset printing industry longer than electronic publishing, which has begun to change everything. Photographs or transparencies were placed on expensive drum scanners that would enlarge or reduce the image to produce the film negatives at the size needed for printing the image in a book, magazine, or catalog. If the image were being used in two different sizes, it had to be scanned twice, once at each size.

Now drum scanners are connected to complex computers that take the same information and digitize it so that the computer can use the original scan again and again at a variety of sizes. The image only needs to be scanned once.

Scanners range in size and quality from handheld scanners and flatbed or desktop scanners to the super-high-resolution drum scanners operated by service bureaus or color houses. The cost of preparing scanned images depends on the quality of the final printing production and the capability of the service bureau to provide color correction on scanned images.

This process is more expensive than Photo CD, but the advantage of using the service bureau for digitizing images comes from the expertise of the scanner operator and the imaging specialist. Together they scan and correct images to achieve the truest color representation and sharpest resolution. The Photo CD operator simply scans the images without evaluating the color correction.

Slide and film scanners have become so sophisticated, however, that only the very high-quality fashion and art publishers use expensive commercial drum scanners. In fact, newspapers and news magazines that for years digitized images with film scanners have shifted to having photographers use high-end digital cameras that can upload images via modem or satellite hookup.

Digital Darkroom Software

Taking the photograph has always been only part of the process of creating a photographic image. The darkroom, where you process and print the film, presents a whole set of challenges for achieving the optimal image. This capability exists in remarkable similarity in the digital environment.

Once the image is brought into the computer—via scanning, Photo CD, or digital camera—you need to assure that when the image is reproduced, it will be true to the original scene it captured. In the computer, you can dodge and burn, perform unsharp masking to sharpen the focus, adjust the color balance or hue saturation, and lighten or darken an entire exposure, much as you would in the traditional darkroom. In the digital darkroom, you have the added ability to lighten only the midtones or only the shadow areas, or to make a number of creative alterations using a wide range of filters. You can see the result on screen instantly, and, if you don't like it, you can change it with the touch of a button.

This capability comes with the computer software. Adobe's Photoshop is the clear leader in the industry, and it includes all the tools you need. It's an extremely complex and powerful program that requires a large investment of time in training—either professional or on your own—and practice to become proficient.

"The gestalt of the photography and computer imaging result in a whole that is greater than the sum of its parts," says Jeff Schewe. "Photoshop allows me to work at an extremely convincing level in terms of altering reality." Schewe is the author of *Photoshop Mastery: The Secrets and Techniques of Jeff Schewe.*

Ethical Issues

The capabilities of the new technology have completely shattered the old saying "a photograph doesn't lie." Although it was possible to make photographs lie with the old technology, now it's possible to create completely seamless, undetectable superimpositions. The ethical question of how much one can alter an image for the sake of aesthetics or some other less noble goal and still maintain the integrity of the image has stirred a lot of controversy.

In the editorial world of journalism—both newspaper and magazine—the line has been drawn quite firmly. A press photographer who asked a firefighter to pose for a photograph was fired for having staged it, for interfering in the representation of truth. Changing the content of an image electronically would also be clear grounds for dismissal.

That's not to say that there isn't room for manipulation of an image in its digital form that remains within the bounds of ethical representation. In the darkroom, the photographer practices a number of techniques to enhance the content of the photograph, not alter it. These are traditional darkroom techniques that in no way compromise the integrity of the photograph's content.

Photographer and designer Jim Williams believes the question of a photograph's integrity has always been not the image itself, but the reputation for reliability of the source of the image.

"When we see a photo in a newspaper," he explains, "we trust not only that it's not faked, but that it reasonably represents the significant parts of the scene because we rely on the journalistic integrity of the newspaper. If we see a glamour photo on a magazine cover, we might exercise a bit more skepticism in deciding to believe that the model is really that gorgeous in real life. And if it's a photo in an ad, well, most of us learn at an early age that the real thing never looks quite as good! If digital imaging has any effect on the believability of photographs, it's simply going to be a matter of throwing the question back onto the reputation of the source, not by asking 'Is that picture real?' so much as 'Can I trust the source of it?' And that's good."

Taking Off on a Digital Career Path

If you're heading for college, look for a school that has developed its computer program in either photojournalism or art photography. The Brooks Institute of Photography in California and the Rochester Institute of Technology in New York both offer extensive programs. The Center for Creative Imaging in Camden, Maine, offers a program of intensive workshops and training created in cooperation with Kodak and the Apple Computer Company. There are many others, and the Internet is a wonderful resource for seeking up-to-date information.

With most states suffering budget cutbacks, not many programs attached to art departments or journalism schools have been able to invest in the expensive equipment required to offer quality instruction in the new digital technology.

Aside from college programs, many computer stores, digital camera manufacturers, and some service bureaus offer training seminars that can get you started. A lot will depend on you. Like learning photography itself, learning to work in the digital environment involves trial and error and repetition for you to become a master image maker.

An internship or apprenticeship with a top-quality prepress service bureau or the digital darkroom of a magazine or newspaper would easily be worth a year's college tuition. You'll learn more quickly working side by side with an expert.

Digital Career Opportunities

There are many career options available that involve the new digital technology and touch on photography as part of the job. In addition, digital technology is an enhancement rather than a requirement in the careers discussed in later chapters. Listed below are some of the areas that involve photography almost exclusively as it relates to the new technology.

Electronic Imaging Specialist. The individual involved with getting photographs into the computer and then preparing them for printing is an electronic imaging specialist. The title may change from job to job, but the work—whether for an advertising agency, a corporation, or a magazine publisher—is similar. A background in photography can be extremely valuable in this position. A knowledge of printing processes and computer-image software is essential.

The imaging specialist receives film, transparencies, or prints from photographers (or, depending on the size of the company, takes the photographs as well), then arranges for the images to be transferred into digital format. This may be done by sending the photos to a Kodak Photo CD processor or to a service bureau that scans the images using a high-resolution drum scanner, or by scanning them in-house on a slide, film, drum, or flatbed scanner.

Once the images are digitized, the specialist uses photo enhancement software to prepare the final image for the final product. The images then go to the graphic designer, who places the images into the electronic layout.

Electronic imaging specialists also work for hospitals, industrial photography studios, printing plants, newspapers, the military, federal and state government agencies, and photofinishers.

Publishing. The electronic revolution has most rapidly been embraced by the magazine and newspaper publishing industries. These industries were the pioneers in early word-processing systems, and they were again quick to see the cost-effectiveness of digital technology.

Many new magazines and newsletters or tabloid papers have sprung up because of the new technology. Desktop publishing systems enabled virtually anyone to become a publisher, as long as there was enough capital to pay for the printer. Many larger publications are already involved with in-house photo imaging. Entire publications are laid out on the computer screen rather than the drafting table.

The book publishing industry has been slower to move to the new technology. It might take some salesmanship to persuade a vice president for design at a major publishing house that the graphics department needs someone in-house to assure quality images in books and on covers. Someone with a thorough understanding of the new technology will have a decided advantage.

Advertising Imaging. Ad agencies and corporate ad departments have moved almost entirely into the digital world. Advertising photographers either use high-caliber digital cameras or digital backs for their large-format traditional cameras. Although the initial investment in equipment is expensive, the savings in processing, darkroom retouching, and film can be recouped rapidly. Traditionally the advertising agency prepared an ad campaign using the same image in a variety of promotional ads, mailers, brochures, or posters. The image would be printed a different size in each, which required rescanning the image to the correct size for each product. Digital technology means that the image is immediately digitized or scanned once at the largest size, if film was used, and then electronically reduced to fit all the other sizes. The result is a tremendous savings in the photographic imaging budget. The time savings is also dramatic. Art directors can see prospective photo layouts within a day or two rather than the weeks required in a traditional setting.

Corporate and Industrial Imaging. Jim Williams works as both an in-house photographer and a graphics specialist for a large consumer-products company. His time is split between computer graphics and taking photographs for the packaging of his company's products. When he shoots photographs, it is with the specific intent of putting them into digital form through Photo CD. He uses a 35 mm camera, and the film goes straight onto CD. "I don't even bother with contact sheets," Jim says. "I've been having good results, both for proofs and printed four-color sales promotion pieces we've done."

Jim also works with other photographers, and he is often frustrated that so many are not yet up to speed with the new technology. "I love to work with a photographer who can say, 'Do you want the chromes, Photo CD, or TIFF files on a jaz disk? Just let me know what you need, and I'll take care of it.' Someone who did that would have a real competitive advantage!"

Service Bureaus. Service bureaus, or color prepress houses, have invested in the expensive technology required to take photographs and digitize the information directly into the computer to allow image editing and the repeated use of an image in printed matter. The jobs in these organizations change as the technology changes, but here are the basics.

The scanner operator must be extremely knowledgeable about the production of color images for printing. The best scanner operators come from a background in traditional color photography. The scanner operator takes the client's film, slides, prints, or transparencies and establishes the specific needs for how the final image will be printed. Knowledge of how different preparations affect the final printed piece is essential.

A scanner operator makes from $25 to $50 per hour, more if the scanner operator also owns the service bureau. Service bureaus charge from $35 to $250 for each scan, depending on its size and the quality or resolution of the scanner, and from $65 to $300 per hour for any retouching work.

The digital imaging specialist or technician works with the scanned image, making the fine-tuning adjustments to assure the ultimate quality of the image's reproduction. This individual can also create "masks" to drop the background out of a photograph of an object or person, as is often done in mail-order catalogs. The specialist is also capable of creating special effects as desired. A digital imaging specialist working for a service bureau earns from $16 to $60 per hour.

Video Editing. Nearly all news broadcast organizations now use computers to edit videotapes that will run during the newscast. The advantages of speed and the ability to program them into computerized video and sound management systems have made this option very attractive. The ability to work with video images in a computer environment also has uses in the corporate and industrial world. Sales presentations, training seminars, and informational presentations can all benefit from a sophisticated blending of multimedia film, sound, text, and still imagery.

A video editor for a broadcast company might expect $14,000 to $40,000 as a staff salary in broadcasting, slightly more in an industry or corporate position.

Stock Photography. Although there was initial concern that the Photo CD revolution would cut deeply into the stock photography market for traditional images, entrepreneurial photographers saw the new technology as an advantage. "Photographers could exploit digital imaging by thinking creatively," Jim Williams suggests. "Digital distribution allows the photographer to create highly targeted collections of special-interest photos and market directly to the photo buyer."

Many stock agencies have moved online. The Kodak Picture Exchange, one of the first global image marketing services, is an online database of thousands of stock photography images. Subscribers to the online service can use a database to search for images by keyword, then order the transparency for publishing from the stock agency at regular rates. Now there are any number of competitors, such as Corbis, Artville, and PictureQuest.

Customers can select images or entire theme-related CDs, complete an order form using a credit card or, for business accounts, a purchase order, then download the high-resolution image ready for inclusion in electronic layouts.

....

For More Information

Organizations
Digital Printing and Imaging Association
10015 Main Street
Fairfax, VA 22031

International Digital Imaging Association
84 Park Avenue
Flemington, NJ 08822

Technical Association of the Graphic Arts
68 Lomb Memorial Drive
Rochester NY 14623

Books

Basic Digital Photography, by Norman Breslow. Butterworth-Heinemann.

Basic Digital Photography: A Comprehensive Step-by-Step Guide to Selecting and Using Digital Cameras, by Ron Eggers. Amherst Media, Inc.

Digital Effects: Jim Zuckerman's Secrets to Great Photographs, by Jim Zuckerman. Writer's Digest Books.

Introduction to Digital Imaging, by Joseph Ciaglia. Prentice Hall.

Photoshop 6 Cookbook, by Dieter Froebisch et al. Silver Pixel Press.

In addition, Kodak has a number of photography-related publications available online at www.kodak.com. The site also offers the online Digital Learning Center.

Periodicals

Digital Photographer Magazine
4880 Market Street
Ventura, CA 93003
www.digiphotomag.com
   (Bimonthly magazine for the amateur digital photographer.)

PC Photo Magazine
12121 Wilshire Boulevard, Twelfth Floor
Los Angeles, CA 90025
www.pcphotomag.com
   (Bimonthly magazine featuring reviews, tips, and stories on all things digital in photography.)

PEI Magazine
229 Peachtree Street NE, Suite 2200
Atlanta, GA 30303
www.peimag.com
   (Monthly magazine dedicated exclusively to electronic imaging, photography, and computer graphics.)

The following publications regularly include sections and articles on the new technology, as well as product reviews:

Photon
Icon Publications
Maxwell Place
Maxwell Lane
Kelso
Roxburghshire TD5 7BB
Scotland, UK
www.photonpub.co.uk
   (Monthly magazine that alternates between professional, 35 mm, and digital editions.)

Professional Photographer
229 Peachtree Street NE, Suite 2200
Atlanta, GA 30303
www.ppmag.com

Shutterbug
5211 South Washington Avenue
Titusville, FL 32780
www.shutterbug.net

CHAPTER THREE

The News Beat

Photojournalism and Press Photography

Virtually every newspaper, no matter how small, employs at least one photographer. That person also may be the paper's editor, reporter, and darkroom technician, but with the notable exception of the *Wall Street Journal,* any newspaper's content includes photographs.

Readers want pictures with captions that tell a story quickly—they often don't have time for more than that. Reader surveys have shown repeatedly that first a reader looks at the photograph, then the caption, then the headline, and then perhaps the first paragraph of the story. The photographer works with the reporter in the desire to "hook" the reader with an interesting photograph, something to entice the reader into reading the story to find out what is happening in the photo.

Photojournalism is essentially reporting with a camera. *Photojournalism* is a term coined to describe the unique merger of pictures and words to present newsworthy information in print media. Toward this end, the photojournalist is as much involved with communication as is the reporter. Whether it's the anguished look of a basketball player who just missed a crucial shot or the triumphant salute of a victorious candidate for the presidency, the photojournalist seeks to capture what Henri Cartier-Bresson called the "decisive moment"—the moment that expresses the heart of the story.

Photography is an elemental part of the design or look of a newspaper. Most photographs provide visual references for

41

particular news stories. Others might be "drop-ins" that provide some welcome relief from column after column of gray type. In an increasingly visual world, the importance of photography in the print media has increased.

Working Conditions

Even when not on assignment or in the darkroom, the photographer of a news organization is on duty. The camera is as much a part of the news photographer's requisite accessories as the notepad and pencil are of the reporter's.

How a news photographer spends the day depends on whether the newspaper is a daily, weekly, or monthly, and if it's published for morning or afternoon distribution. A photojournalist also may work for one of the major news bureaus, such as the Associated Press or Knight-Ridder.

What the photographer shoots depends on the size of the paper. The larger the paper, the more opportunity for the photographer to specialize in an area such as sports or features. With a smaller paper, it's more likely that assignments will range from covering local school board meetings and high school basketball games to being on the scene of a four-alarm fire.

Variety Is the Spice of a Photojournalist's Life

A staff photographer might cover any and all of the following subject areas:

- Advertising
- Business and industry
- Celebrity photos
- Documentary photo essays
- Fashion
- Features
- Food
- Home and real estate

- Photo illustration
- Planned event coverage
- Public relations (the newspaper's PR)   ·
- Sports
- Spot news

Sports is a subject that gets many beginning photographers into the news business. Usually the fascination starts in high school or college when you're sitting on the sidelines watching the game, maybe with camera in hand, and you manage to shoot a fantastic picture of the quarterback catching the winning pass in the end zone. The thrill is infectious and tenacious, and it keeps many a photographer working hard to repeat the significant moment.

Sports is also a source of freelance work. Staff photographers often can't cover everything, especially with the increasing popularity of women's sports and once lesser-known sports such as soccer and rugby. A freelancer who manages to snap some telling photos at these events has a good chance of making a sale.

The Daily Newspaper Routine

Mark Crummett began his career as a photographer for the forty-five-thousand-circulation *Frederick News-Post*, a community daily newspaper in Maryland. "We cover the community like a blanket," Mark says. "If it doesn't happen in Frederick County, it doesn't happen for us. Our managing editor tells people, 'if you want to know what happened in Bosnia, read the *Washington Post.*'"

The *News-Post* photographers get their assignments from an assignments editor. This person fields calls from people wanting their pictures in the paper, then logs the information into the assignment book. Photographers check the book when they come on shift, then get assignment forms that specify who and what to photograph. If needed, they check with the reporter, editor, or subject of the photograph for more information. Sometimes Mark works directly with the reporters to provide shots for their stories.

All five staff photographers at the *News-Post* shoot for the business, agriculture, food, and family/entertainment sections of the newspaper. They also shoot for the advertising department and for internal communications such as the company directory.

"For me, one of the great things about working at a newspaper is that almost every day is different," says Mark. "Certainly there are the perennial assignments, things that come up every year—the fair, fund-raising events and their promos, new organization officers. But we get to shoot a lot of different things."

When there aren't assignments on the book, or between assignments, photographers often cruise for feature photos—wildlife, art, enterprise, slice-of-life photos that show what's going on in the area. "These are probably the best part of the job for me," says Mark. "They give me an excuse to walk up to total strangers and say, 'Hey, what ya doin'?'"

While out of the office, each of the photographers on the *News-Post* carries a two-way radio to be able to contact other photographers and the newsroom to report spot news (events occurring "on the spot," such as automobile accidents or police actions) or to check on assignments. "These have really come in handy for things like presidential visits," Mark explains. "George Bush occasionally played golf near here, and Camp David is in the northern end of Frederick County."

The Pressure of Deadlines. On a daily paper, deadlines are set throughout the day to meet various printing times for editions of the paper. A late-breaking story may mean getting an assignment at 10:00 P.M., driving across town to shoot the story, and returning to develop and print in time to put photos on the editor's desk by 11:30 P.M. A daily paper scheduled for afternoon delivery might have deadlines at 4:00 A.M. and again at 7:00 A.M. and 10:00 A.M.

At the *News-Post*, at least one photographer is on duty from 7:00 A.M. to 10:30 P.M. every day, and the chief photographer usually listens to a police scanner at night. The late-shift photographer is responsible for covering sports, usually local high school or collegiate events. After shooting the first half of the game, the photographer often returns to the darkroom to develop film and scan the photos for the next day's paper.

Darkroom Duties. During the last half of his shift, Mark returns to the office to process film and write captions. At most newspapers, photographers are responsible for doing their own darkroom work. This may mean mixing chemicals, developing film, and making prints or halftones for traditional layout, but most likely it means scanning the developed film or uploading images from a digital camera into the computer. Then the photographer works the standard darkroom magic but in a digital environment, using Adobe Photoshop or a comparable image-editing software to dodge and burn, apply filters to achieve better contrast or color balance, or sharpen. Larger newspapers often have staff people who handle the darkroom work, which leaves the photographers free to do what they do best—take pictures.

Working with the Photo Editor. Once the photographer has developed the film and made a preliminary selection of photographs, it's time for the photo editor, if the paper's large enough to have one on staff, to make the final selections. The photo editor might also provide feedback about the photographs in terms of overall quality and how they might be improved—whether by a different choice of angle, filter, lens, exposure, or focus.

The Weekly Routine

The pace at a weekly paper revolves around one deadline each week. The photographer will most likely be assigned to cover local meetings, school sports, and the standard grip-and-grin shot of the mayor handing over the key of the city to a visiting dignitary. In addition, the editor may assign some photography for a forthcoming feature story, or the ad director may need a few shots of the new grocery store in town for an advertising spread.

It's not uncommon to see events, people, or scenes of interest on the way to work, but once at the paper's offices, the photographer picks up assignments from the photo editor. There may be several assignments, some for immediate action, some for next week's deadline. The photographer then works with the reporter to get familiar with the story, schedules the shoot, and develops and scans the film.

Jenna Calk is staff photographer for two weekly papers in Oregon. She works as the primary photographer for one of the papers and handles all the darkroom work for the other. She works four days a week and has the freedom to develop her own story ideas.

Jenna believes that working for weekly papers offers several advantages over working for most dailies. Deadlines are more relaxed, which allows time for creativity and thoroughness. "If I find out that we're missing the name of a player on the football shot, I have a couple of days to run out and get the player's name," Jenna explains. "Also there's a lot of freedom for special projects. If I come up with an idea and the editor buys it, I may end up with a full-page photo story. On a daily, you have to lobby a lot more aggressively to get half that space."

As the only photographer on staff, Jenna likes the fact that she gets all the assignments. She doesn't have to take only the grip-and-grin shots while someone else gets to attend a celebrity event.

"I would like to move to a daily paper, but I'm also realizing how competitive it is," she admits. "I've been doing this since I graduated from college. I've applied to a lot of jobs, but I'm married and like this area, so there aren't a lot of options."

The Monthly Tabloid Routine

Many monthly publications straddle the line between newspapers and magazines. Their content includes both news and features, and most are in small communities that are not served by a major daily. Most are too small to have more than one photographer.

Bob McEowen works as staff photographer—and sometimes writer, designer, and editor—for a monthly statewide newspaper published by a regional utility company. Combining responsibilities for writing and photography, as well as decisions about what does and does not appear in the newspaper, has changed the way he looks at photojournalism.

Bob had worked as a newspaper photographer but felt there was something missing. "When I was a news photographer, I was pretty much an order filler," he explains. "Now I believe I am truly a photojournalist. Not only do I do it all now, but I have more freedom than I did when working for a newspaper."

What It Takes to Be a Photojournalist

Speed, Flexibility, and Grit

Photographers who work for daily papers must be able to work quickly and efficiently to meet their deadlines. With any newspaper, photographers must be ready to be sent out on a breaking story any time of day or night. They have to be quick, agile, and capable of carrying a heavy camera bag for long hauls.

Photojournalists covering wars or civil unrest, natural disasters, or feature stories that take them into dangerous segments of society have to face the possibility of personal injury or even death. When I was in London in 1993, a photographer whose newspaper had been tipped off to a bomb threat in the financial district was killed as he wandered the virtually empty street seeking a photograph. The bomb blew out several buildings—I felt the trembling force of it several miles away—but the press photographer was the only person killed. More recently, several photographers have lost their lives while caught in the deadly wars of the Middle East.

Photographers might have to face deeply moving or tragic situations that they capture on film, and it can be difficult to develop and print the film without reliving some of the agony of the experiences.

People Skills and Persistence

Working with people and getting information from them is a central part of the photojournalist's job. Curiosity helps reporters and photographers alike when it comes to digging beneath the surface for the information to make a story or image more newsworthy. Persistence pays off when subjects prove elusive or uncooperative.

Preparation: One Photographer's Adventure

Photographers must be prepared for all eventualities in this business. Mark Crummett, then with the *Frederick News-Post,* went to photograph a rescue from an icebound home far back in the Maryland woods. A man had fallen while walking the dog and hurt his leg. His wife fell trying to help him, breaking her ankle. It took her two hours to drag herself back up the icy road to their home, where she called rescue personnel.

Mark arrived at the scene after the first truck had gone in. He followed, picking his way over the ice-covered road through the woods, falling a couple of times. With the first fall, he broke his radio, which left him unable to contact the newspaper. A second fall broke the bulb in his flash. A state helicopter was circling and lighting the area, but the wildly moving shadows from its search light made photographing without his own lighting difficult.

As he approached, Mark slid down the road a couple of hundred feet to the scene, where he found a crew of firefighters working their way up the road on the other side of the valley, roped together and hacking footholds in the inch-thick ice with an ax. There was nowhere to stand except where they had chopped—any misstep would send him sliding to the bottom of the hill.

As the firefighters mountaineered up the hillside, Mark started taking photos of the chopping-and-roping routine. After one frame, he heard a familiar groan from his camera—the batteries were dying fast in the subfreezing air. He was in the middle of a dramatic rescue, a mile from anywhere with no way out and no means of reporting to the paper, in the dark, with no flash.

"I suddenly remembered that I had my brand new Nikon Litetouch in a case on my belt!" Mark realized. "I was saved!"

He continued up the hill with the rescue workers and photographed them sliding the woman out her front door in a stokes basket and down the hill to the rescue truck. And, thanks to a coworker, the film made it out in time for the shots to appear on the front page of the next morning's paper.

The Digital Darkroom

Computer skills are a must, and familiarity with digital cameras is increasingly important. Like most industries, the newspaper business has been radically altered by the development of computer and satellite technology. The hands-on work of putting a newspaper together has shifted to the electronic environment of computers, scanners, modems, and image setters.

At the *News-Post*, photographs are scanned into computers rather than turned into halftones in the darkroom, and the composing room—formerly staffed by typesetters working at desk-sized compositors—is now equipped with desktop computers.

Photographers working for news bureaus and larger metropolitan daily newspapers have, willingly or not, had to come to terms with the digital revolution in photography. A laptop computer, portable scanner, and modem are standard equipment for a photographer traveling on assignment, and a majority now use digital cameras that can upload images directly to the computer.

After scanning film or uploading from a digital camera, the photographer sends it electronically to the photo editor, who might crop it Photoshop before sending it to the layout department. Once layout is complete, the composited file is downloaded to the printing plant—no more rushing wet prints to the layout department or driving pasteups across town to the printer. When the newspaper is "put to bed," it's with the touch of a button. Chapter 2 presents a more detailed discussion of technology.

Kelly Richmond, who works as a stringer for the Associated Press and several daily newspapers, says that a digital camera and a means of instant transmission to the newspaper—such as a satellite cell phone—is a must for photojournalists who work on tight deadlines or with breaking news stories. The amount of time needed to shoot the image and get it to the news desk is compressed to a matter of minutes rather than hours.

Photojournalists working on their own may find the cost of high-tech equipment prohibitive. The price of professional-caliber digital cameras remains high, despite decreasing prices in the consumer market. The systems capable of rapidly transferring large graphic files to news bureaus via modem or satellite link are also expensive. Some photojournalists, however, suggest that a high-quality film scanner and communications software can work well and reduce the cost for essentially the same result, with the only loss being processing and transmission speed.

Communication with Words

Communicating with photographs in a newspaper involves more than just shooting pictures. You need to develop a "nose for news." What makes a good story, both visually and in print? Is it new? Is it timely? Is there a human interest angle? Does it capture local interest? Your photos will tell most of the story, but you also need to be prepared to gather some facts to go along with them.

Photo Captions. Most newspapers require their photographers to provide full caption information when submitting their photographs. That means getting the five Ws of journalism answered with as much information as possible. Not all of it will be used in the caption, but it's better to err on the side of too much information than not enough. If you don't get a contact name and number, you'll never be able to go back to the subject of the photo to fill in the gaps in your information. The five Ws of journalism form the basic building blocks of any news story.

- **Who.** To satisfy this element, you need to get all the names of the individuals appearing in the photograph. When getting names, it's essential to get correct spellings and any initials or additions, such as Jr. or Sr., to help specifically identify each individual. Addresses can also be important identifying information.
- **What.** What's happening in the photograph? Use active, present-tense verbs to describe the action of the image: a fire burns out of control, the mayor addresses a crowded news conference, the players run onto the field. The action of the image is the center point of a strong photo caption.

- **When.** *When* is an important element for most photographs in news publications. While a story on the state's senator might run with a file photo, a story on a political rally for a senator would need to include a photo of the event itself. A newspaper isn't interested in running a photo that isn't new, even if it's just a "passing scenes" shot to break up an otherwise gray news page.
- **Where.** The degree of specificity required about the location of a photo setting depends on the situation. Is the subject of the photograph in a courtroom? Fishing along the Muskogee River? Boarding a plane bound for Rio? Maybe you need to indicate that the car in which the subject is photographed is a police car on its way to the county jail. Often the *where* of an image will be irrelevant in the final caption, but as with the other elements, it should be included in the complete caption that you turn in with the photo.
- **Why.** Many photo captions don't address the question of *why* an action took place, although it can be important to explain what's going on in a photograph. The caption for Mark Crummett's picture of an emergency rescue worker chopping footholds into an icy hillside might include the *why* element for clarification: to rescue a couple injured by falls on the ice.

Accuracy and Ethics

Newspapers absolutely hate to print retractions, so it's vitally important to get your information right the first time. In addition, photographers are often confronted with situations that require a strong grounding in ethics to handle appropriately. In an age where photographs can so easily be altered, it's essential for news photographers to represent truth—and only truth—in their photographs. That means you don't remove a piece of litter that mars an otherwise perfect photo of the governor. It's a matter of assuring that your photographs provide true and accurate representations of the news.

Photographers also sometimes confront the moral dilemma of whether to take a photograph or to respect an individual's need or right to privacy. Most news organizations have clear standards and practices outlined for their employees that cover sensitive issues and how they should be handled. Journalism ethics courses are another excellent source of basic ethics knowledge.

Other Useful Skills

The ability to speak a foreign language is a big asset for photographers working for larger papers, in metropolitan areas, or on travel assignments. A photographer who speaks fluent Spanish, for example, will have a significant edge on the competition for a staff job in Los Angeles or an assignment to follow the president on a goodwill tour to Mexico.

Read the newspaper—the one you want to work for especially, as well as other papers you admire—to gain insight into what the editors are doing with photographs, how the photos relate to the stories they accompany, and how the work you do would fit with the image a newspaper presents. You'll make yourself valuable to your editors if you consistently deliver photos that work specifically for your newspaper.

Being an "idea person" is also a major asset in getting assignments, especially on publications that have a lot of space to fill every day. Editors appreciate people who can develop ideas on their own and then follow them through to the publishable finish. Newspapers are also a terrific source for story ideas that can help you get published if you haven't yet made a staff connection.

Getting Started

The most important decision you have to make before setting out to begin a career as a photojournalist is whether photography and journalism, together, are what you would truly love to do. "If you are planning to pursue a career in photojournalism, then you should make sure that journalism is in your blood and you love it, because, frankly, you are not going to get rich doing it," writes Nancy L. Ford in her essay, "Photojournalism as a Career."

Nancy, photo editor of the *Observer-Dispatch* in Syracuse, New York, studied commercial photography at Syracuse University. She began working at the *Observer-Dispatch* part-time. "I took the job for only one reason," she recalls, "because it was the only job I could get where I could make money doing photography. My first day on the job, I was driving around town with a two-way radio and police scanner and found myself chasing fires and other news. My whole world changed that day. I knew I was in love.

"I make an issue of this because I have had many interns who come to work for us, who work their shift and go home. They never brought photographs that they shot for themselves, on their own time. Or even worse, they are photojournalism majors who do not know how to use a flash or how to operate their cameras in the manual mode (thus not fully understanding f-stops, shutter speed, TTL or, most important, how and why the camera, which is the tool of the trade, works).

"I had an intern who was a photojournalism major at Syracuse University. For a whole summer he worked for us twenty hours a week and never suggested one photo story. Every day that he worked, at the end of his shift he was in a hurry, running out the door to meet his girlfriend. When fall approached and he was getting ready to go back to school, I asked him if he had shot anything all summer on his own time that was not for work. His eyes dropped to the floor and he said, 'No.'"

Nancy's essay, available online at www.nlford.com, provides more information about a photojournalist's responsibilities as well as a lot of good advice on how to approach photo editors in your job search.

Education

To become a photojournalist, your most important assets will be your thorough knowledge of your camera and the ability to to take great photos, your sense for what makes a great photograph, and your understanding of what makes a photograph newsworthy. To gain these skills, most photographers need to receive training, whether formal or informal. In today's hiring market, the photographer with a bachelor's degree or a graduate degree will have an edge in an interview, portfolios being equal. Degrees in journalism, history, political science, or art are all good starting places for careers in photojournalism. Because of its strong emphasis on communication, journalism is a natural fit that provides valuable insight into the workings of the news industry and the job of a reporter.

The American Society of Newspaper Editors (ASNE) conducted a survey of its members and found that a degree in journalism, as opposed to other subject areas, gave job applicants a significant advantage at the majority of small newspapers, which is where most photojournalists begin their careers.Whether you major in journalism or another liberal arts subject, the society suggests that you broaden your background by taking courses in many fields.

While you're in school, in college or in high school, work for the school newspaper. According to the ASNE survey, such experience adds a great deal to your desirability as a job candidate.

Internships

Most editors agree that internships are the best way to begin a career in journalism. If you're still in high school, you might investigate the possibility of job shadowing, following a photographer or photo editor around for a day or two. If you're in college, the opportunities are considerably more extensive. Paid internships are, of course, most attractive, but experience is the real goal of an internship.

Jumping into Photojournalism

Dan McComb, who held an internship at the *Spokane Spokesman-Review,* among others, started his career in photojournalism in a dramatic but roundabout fashion.

"When I was about eighteen, my main mission in life was figuring out how to pay for a ski season pass," he explains. He took up fighting forest fires during the summer for the U.S. Forest Service, eventually working his way into the elite smoke-jumping ranks. "One particularly grueling day, I found myself looking down as I drifted toward a patch of jagged rocks and burning trees, and I thought to myself: 'This is pretty ridiculous. Nobody would believe it!'" He decided to start carrying a camera with him, and after a couple of seasons he found he was spending more time working the shutter than working the fire line.

A broken back and pelvis on a fire jump made a career change necessary. He went to the University of Montana's School of Journalism, then won a scholarship to study photojournalism in London with a former *National Geographic* director of photography.

Following graduation, Dan worked as an intern for papers in Montana, Michigan, and Tennessee. His experience attests to the high level of competition in this fast-paced area of photography. "I had no idea it would be this tough to get a 'real' job," Dan says. "Internships come easy because newspapers don't have to pay you benefits. But they're great experiences, so I'll probably bounce around from paper to paper until somebody gives me a place to hang my hat." But he didn't get discouraged. "In photojournalism, as in smoke jumping, it pays to keep an airborne attitude."

Advice from the Pros

Shoot, Shoot, Shoot

As with any field in photography, the key element to success is taking pictures. Shoot all the time, then go into the darkroom and develop, print, and see what you've got.

Mark Crummett's advice is to keep a camera (or several) with you all the time. As one of his editors once said, "When in doubt, take lots of pictures. Shoot anything the paper may be interested in," he adds. "The worst that could happen is they won't use it. Our paper doesn't use freelancers for assignments, but we will run just about anything they send in for local organizations."

Build a Dynamite Portfolio

Your portfolio is your calling card. It's what will open doors and bring you assignments and jobs. But it won't do any of that unless it shows that you've got what it takes to turn pro. It should represent both your technical ability and your aesthetic sensibility. For more guidelines on portfolio photos, see Chapters 7 and 12.

In addition to the photographs, your portfolio should include a resume that lists your education and experience, and a brief but informative cover letter that expresses your interests and highlights the pertinent aspects of your experience. When sending a portfolio by mail, be sure to address it to a specific individual by name, usually the photo editor, and include an appropriately sized self-addressed, stamped envelope. Be sure you've made no mistakes in the name, address, or anything in your letter or resume. Remember that accuracy is a key characteristic for a journalist!

Find a Mentor

Mark Crummett suggests buddying up with photographers at the local newspaper. The newspaper may not have any openings available, but the photographers can often tell you about jobs at other papers. They'll also probably be happy to comment on your work; however, Mark cautions, "be prepared for some honesty!"

Jamilla Robinson, who works for the Newspaper Association of America, counsels students to write freelance articles, shadow local reporters, or invite a professional journalist for a cup of coffee. "Learn something new in journalism," she adds; "take a risk. Success doesn't come from luck; it is a combination of hard work, integrity, commitment, and even some fun, so make it happen."

Learn the Technology

Your most important tool, of course, is your camera, and you must know it inside and out. Understand all the film speed settings and how different settings affect photographs in different lighting conditions; know all its special-effects options and what they mean for taking the best possible images; know how to maintain it for optimum performance. With the growing importance of digital technology in the news world, it's also essential to gain skill and experience working with computers and photo-editing software. And, even though digital darkrooms are fast becoming the norm, you should also know your way around a traditional darkroom—how to mix chemicals, develop film, and make prints using a variety of filters and techniques to achieve optimal results.

Finding Your Opportunities

As Green Bay Packers coach Vince Lombardi told his players, "Luck, that's where preparation meets opportunity." Being prepared, for the photojournalist, means that the camera or cameras are within easy reach, are loaded with film or memory cards, and have charged batteries. Being prepared also means the photojournalist is always looking for the defining moment.

With 1,573 daily newspapers and 9,269 weekly or monthly community newspapers published in the United States alone, the opportunities for photographers in this field are broad. Photojournalism is one aspect of photography that is not limited geographically. A town doesn't have to be very large to warrant having its own newspaper, and it's at these small-town weekly papers that beginning photojournalists may find their first real breaks.

Starting in the Darkroom

You might begin a career in newspaper photography in the darkroom—traditional or digital—spending six months working on developing and printing film shot by others. Use that time to critique the work you see, figure out how the good shots were taken, what it is that makes them compelling or informative. Work with the photo editor to learn what kinds of photographs typically are run in the newspaper, what that particular paper looks for in its photography, and why.

Working as an Assistant

Your next step may be to serve as assistant to a veteran photographer, going out on assignments and helping to gather information or change film in cameras. Such an experience can help you learn the protocol for working your way into situations to get the best photographs, getting the information you need for captions, working at crime or accident scenes around medical or law enforcement personnel, and so forth.

Working as a Stringer

In newspaper jargon, a "stringer" is someone newspapers use to cover stories the staff photographers can't get to. Most stringers don't live in the same town in which the paper is published. They are called upon to cover local events when the paper doesn't have a staff photographer to send. If you prove your worth, you can eventually work your way into a staff position or gather enough clips in the meantime to apply to other newspapers. Stringers are generally paid by the day or the assignment.

Persistence Pays. When Jenna Calk began looking for work, it was persistence that finally made the payoff. In addition to doing all the freelance work she could round up, she called all the area newspapers and spoke with the photo editors. If there were no openings, she asked to show her work anyway.

"I wasn't always warmly received," she says. "Once I asked someone if I could stop in with my portfolio and he said, 'Don't bother, you'd be wasting your time and ours.'"

The editor of the state capital's city newspaper, who agreed to look at Jenna's work but had no assignments to offer, later recommended her to a colleague at a nearby weekly paper who needed someone in a hurry.

"The editor of the weekly called and asked if I could please come down to the paper and make some prints," Jenna recalls. "His staff photographer had just walked out and the deadline was approaching. He said we would discuss the possibility of his hiring me permanently later. So I worked several hours that day making prints. We chatted informally, and he ended up asking me to take the job."

Opportunities for Advancement

There's a limited amount of upward mobility in the field of newspaper photography. As a working press photographer, your ultimate goal might be to get glamour jobs, such as covering the campaign trail of a presidential candidate for the *Washington Post* or being assigned to the Paris bureau of the Associated Press. For the photojournalism elite, cities such as New York, Washington, Boston, Chicago, or Los Angeles are merely jumping-off points for even more exotic and often more dangerous locations, such as Afghanistan, Bosnia-Herzogovina, or the Persian Gulf.

Major newspapers might list a senior vice president–art, a position that might be held by someone who started out in the newspaper's darkroom. Any daily newspaper and some larger weeklies have a photo editor on staff.

Photograph Production Supervisor

On a large newspaper, the darkroom needs to have someone in charge to get the film processed, scanned, and fine-tuned in time to meet the paper's deadline. This individual may rise from among the ranks of the newspaper photographers but is more likely to be someone who has worked in the darkroom for some time and has little desire to work in the field as a press photographer.

Assistant Photo Editor

The next logical in-house position for a photographer is assistant photo editor. This person works with the photo editor, handling everything from communicating assignments to staff photographers to archiving film negatives. The assistant also might be responsible for pulling photographs from past issues for use by other newspapers or for historical features, such as the "year in review" issue that many papers publish around New Year's Day.

Photo Editor or Chief Photographer

The photo editor meets daily with the editors to determine special photographic needs for the paper, then makes assignments to staff photographers. A finely tuned sense of newsworthiness, gained, most likely, from years of experience as a press photographer, is an essential requirement for the person who decides what image appears on the newspaper's cover and section pages.

The photo editor or chief photographer is responsible for checking photographers' contact sheets and selecting the images to be printed for publication, often choosing a vertical and a horizontal version of the same subject to give the graphics layout department an option as the page spreads are created.

Freelancers who want to submit work to the newspaper or hope to gain assignments should apply to the photo editor, who also hires photographers for staff positions.

According to Nancy Ford, of the *Observer-Dispatch,* "Being a photo editor is one of the toughest jobs in the newsroom. The position is a combination of many occupations rolled into one: photographer, editor, lab technician, mentor, mother (or father), friend, diplomat, brainstormer, accountant, inventory clerk, bargain hunter, systems manager, architect, repair person, traffic cop, coach, and cheerleader. It's all a balancing act, which usually leads to burning a lot of energy to make a lot of people happy."

She outlines the following responsibilities of a newspaper photo editor:

- Discuss photo assignments to make sure photographers clearly understand the angle of the story and the types of opportunities to look for while on assignment
- Edit film and critique how the photographer approached the assignment
- Sift through story budgets looking for stories that would lend themselves to great photos
- Attend planning meetings
- Talk to editors and reporters about the stories and write up photo assignments, sometimes with the reporters
- Schedule photographers' shifts and juggle photo assignments with their schedules

- Talk with the design desk about size, crop, and place for a photo in the paper
- Educate and train staff members
- Motivate staff and handle annual performance reviews
- Handle complaints from editors, readers, or others
- Assure that camera, photo processing equipment, computers, and scanners remain in top working order
- Deal with money ("squeezing blood" from a supply budget)
- Write proposals to obtain new or updated equipment

"Most newspapers have limited resources," Nancy adds. That means there are often not enough photographers to handle all the assignments, which increases the pressure on everyone. Her job is to provide interesting opportunities for the photographers while satisfying the photo needs of metro, features, sports, business, and lifestyle departments. "The secret to being a good photo editor is not to alienate one person when giving to another."

Managing Editor: Graphics

The professional at this level oversees not only a staff of photographers, but an entire crew of designers, pasteup artists, and production people. The managing editor for graphics is responsible for the "look" of the paper.

Photographers and designers are equally likely to achieve the rank of graphics managing editor. Both are involved with visual communication, and both will have had several years of experience in the newspaper business.

Income Potential

Newspaper salaries depend on both union contracts and the size and geographic location of the paper itself. Salaries are higher in the more densely populated Northeast and in larger metropolitan areas. Staff photographers earn an average of $28,660. According to the News Guild's 2001 salary survey, top minimum salaries—

the minimum a photographer under contract would earn after about five years on the job—ranged from a low of $387 per week at a small newspaper in the Midwest to a high of $1,384 per week for the *New York Times*. Photographers often were given an additional allowance if they provided their own equipment.

An average starting salary for an assistant photo editor is approximately $25,000. Photo editors earn between $21,000 and $67,000. Salaries at the managing editor level generally exceed $50,000 per year but vary with geographic location, newspaper circulation size, and longevity with the paper.

Newsmagazines and Other Magazines

Unlike newspapers, few magazines have large photography crews; however, they do provide some staff opportunities. Magazines usually have a list of several freelancers they work with regularly, but the person making the photo assignments is usually a photographer with a photo editor's title and responsibilities. Some very large magazines and magazines that rely heavily on a specific type of photography have staff photographers. *National Geographic*, for example, has a crew of more than thirty-five photographers.

Staff Photographer

Salaried magazine photographers working for weekly newsmagazines must be prepared to travel at a moment's notice, often into dangerous situations. For many photojournalists, a regular position with such a magazine represents the peak of success.

Other magazines do not offer the same level of excitement—or financial reward. The salary of a typical magazine staffer starts at between $14,000 and $19,200; an average salary would be $26,400. Very large magazines with photographers on staff usually have a darkroom and processing facility on-site, which provides job opportunities for a film processor or printer. Although it may seem like a long way to a shooting job, just getting in the door of some of these magazines can be pretty difficult.

Photo Editor

Every magazine that uses photographs in its editorial pages—from *People* and *House Beautiful* to *Rolling Stone* and *Hot Rod News*—has a photo editor on staff. Whether that person is called the managing editor for graphics or the graphics editor, the responsibilities of the position include making sure the magazine has the photographs it needs to put the issue to the press.

The photo editor makes assignments to staff photographers or freelancers based on meetings with the editors who determine the magazine's editorial content. Photo editors also can take advantage of their authority and give themselves the most desirable assignments. Look at it this way: if the magazine is going to pay someone to cover a weeklong festival on a Caribbean island, are you going to send a freelancer or go yourself?

In addition to the obvious benefits of the position, the photo editor also makes more money than the photographer. An average starting salary for a magazine photo editor is $21,000, $30,000 after five years, and $67,000 for photo editors with senior-level responsibilities.

Photojournalists in Broadcast News

Although this book focuses on careers for still photographers, a chapter on photojournalism would be incomplete without a discussion of broadcast news media. The visuals you see on the evening news programs—cable or network or local—were provided by photojournalists. News photographers are more than just camera operators. They have to possess the same "nose for news," the same strong sense of ethics, and the same understanding of the role of the news media in society that reporters and newspaper photographers must have. Sometimes called electronic news gathering (ENG), the work of broadcast photojournalists is very similar to newspaper photography. They work as part of a team with reporters. They must be able to think and act quickly to respond to live news events. And they must deal with the pressure of daily—sometimes hourly—deadlines. Many work in digital format and use satellite connections or microwave vans to transmit footage for instant access to the television broadcasters.

Here are a couple of recent advertisements for television news photojournalists that give insight into what the job is like and what skills are required.

HELP WANTED: PHOTOGRAPHER

The primary focus of the photographer is to shoot and edit videotape under extreme deadline pressure. Insures sound and picture quality of all stories shot. Works alone or with a reporter or field producer to edit the story for air. Operates, as need dictates, ENG microwave van. Maintains inventory of all assigned equipment and is responsible for its upkeep. Examines, maintains, and performs routine maintenance of any assigned vehicle. Performs other duties as assigned. Ability to shoot videotape in all kinds of settings and edit shot tape under deadline. Ability to operate ENG microwave van, drive vehicle, operate VTRs and set up tripods. Knowledge of how cameras work to perform minor repairs and maintenance (unlock jammed tapes, etc.) in field, if necessary. Must possess a valid state driver's license. A minimum of two years' work experience. Dexterity to operate camera, VTR. Vision to shoot and edit videotape. Ability to lift one hundred pounds or more, as needed, of equipment consisting of camera, VTRs, tapes, tripods, batteries, etc. Ability to get into nooks, crannies, and high places to shoot video. Works in all kinds of weather conditions.

HELP WANTED: PHOTOGRAPHER FOR LOCAL TV NEWS

The position is responsible for gathering news video and audio and editing daily news stories. Set up live shots for broadcasts, operate remote vehicles, and contribute news story ideas. Must be able to work flexible days and hours.

Excellent communication skills and ability to work alone under pressure. Must be able to work under deadline pressure. A good driving record required. College degree in related field preferred.

News photographers work long and irregular hours and must be ready to roll at a moment's notice. If covering major events, they often travel to where the news happens. Like their newspaper counterparts, they might find themselves covering anything from the local mayor's press conference to a war-torn country halfway across the globe.

The advice for gaining training and experience as a broadcast photojournalist is the same as described for newspaper professionals: know your equipment, develop an eye for what makes great news footage, learn as much as you can about journalism as a profession, and shoot, shoot, shoot. Many universities offer programs in photojournalism that include videography. Employers in the news media look first for camera operators with a good eye and exceptional technical understanding of the equipment they use, but a college degree is a definite hiring advantage.

Most broadcast photojournalists work as salaried employees of local, network, or cable news programs. Some are self-employed but under contract to television stations. Larger metropolitan areas provide the greatest opportunity for employment, but many broadcast photojournalists begin as in-studio camera operators with small local television stations.

Competition is always keen for jobs in broadcast television news, but demand is expected to grow faster than the average for all occupations through 2010. According to a survey by the Radio-Television News Directors Association (RTNDA), television news photographers earned between a minimum of $13,000 and a maximum of $127,000 in 2000. The average was $27,900. Approximately 17 percent of TV news photographers work under contract with their stations.

For More Information

Organizations
American Society of Media Photographers (ASMP)
150 North Second Street
Philadelphia, PA 19106
www.asmp.org
> *(Publishes monthly* ASMP Bulletin *and provides extensive member services.)*

Associated Press (AP)
50 Rockefeller Plaza
New York, NY 10020
www.ap.org

National Press Photographers Association (NPPA)
3200 Croasdaile Drive, Suite 306
Durham, NC 27705
www.nppa.com
> *(Publishes monthly magazine; offers job information bank for job postings; offers additional services for staff and nonstaff professional press photographers.)*

United States Senate Press Photographers' Gallery (USSPPG)
S-317, The Capitol
Washington, DC 20510
www.senate.gov/galleries/photo

White House News Photographers Association (WHNPA)
7119 Ben Franklin Station
Washington, DC 20044
www.whnpa.org

Books

Associated Press Guide to Photojournalism, by Brian Horton. McGraw-Hill Professional.

Digital Photojournalism, by Susan C. Zavoina et al. Allyn & Bacon, Incorporated.

Photojournalism: The Visual Approach, by Frank P. Hoy. Prentice-Hall.

Photojournalism: The Professionals' Approach, by Kenneth Kobre. Butterworth-Heinemann.

Photojournalism: An Introduction, by Fred Parrish. Wadsworth Publishing.

Periodicals

American Journalism Review
4716 Pontiac Street, Suite 310
College Park, MD 20740

Columbia Journalism Review
Columbia University
700A Journalism Building
New York, NY 10027

Folio: The Magazine for Magazine Management
11 River Bend Road South
Stamford, CT 06907
www.demographics.com
> *(Magazine, published sixteen times annually, featuring trends in the magazine industry.)*

News Photographer
NPPA
3200 Croasdaile Drive, Suite 306
Durham, NC 27705
www.nppa.org/members/magazine/default.htm
> *(Monthly tabloid newspaper published by the NPPA.)*

CHAPTER FOUR

Say Cheese
Portrait and People Photography

Portraiture has a long history, far longer than photography, though the two have been a natural combination since Louis Daguerre, a painter and inventor of the daguerreotype, made his first photographic portraits on metal plates. An invaluable part of historic and sociologic records, portrait photography catalogs social history and human experience, including people both famous and ordinary.

Careers in portraiture range from working as a staff photographer for a large or chain portrait studio to freelancing as an event photographer. The essential ingredient for a portrait photographer, whatever your venue, is an ability to work with the people you photograph. Portraiture offers an accessible, though competitive, opportunity for entrepreneurship, as well as a great base of experience for an aspiring photographer.

Working with, and Pleasing, the Client

The most important skill for a successful portrait photographer, says Marilyn Sholin, a successful studio owner in Florida, is "a genuine interest in people, an ability to work with a variety of people, a willingness to please a client, and an ability to sell a quality product." Pleasing the client means understanding that success doesn't always include the freedom to follow your own artistic vision—not until you are someone like Annie Liebowitz or Richard Avedon taking pictures of celebrities.

Are You Cut Out to Be a Portrait Photographer?

- Do you enjoy working with people all day?
- Are you good at making people feel comfortable?
- Do you have the patience to deal well with the unexpected—crying babies, shy toddlers, grim-faced octogenarians?
- Do you have a genuine interest in discovering and satisfying the client's wishes?
- Do you have an aptitude for the details of business—filing, record keeping, billing, and marketing?

Getting Started

As you begin a career in portrait photography, you have many options for gaining the experience you need to become an independent professional. Portrait studios sometimes work with educational institutions to provide internships for students. Often chain studios or department store studios will hire inexperienced photographers and put them through on-the-job training programs. If you're willing to start by working as an assistant for a small business or doing support work for a professional portrait studio photographer, you are likely to gain valuable experience.

There are, of course, many photography courses and programs of study at colleges, universities, and art schools. Portraiture specializations in professional photography programs will likely include courses such as portraiture fundamentals, lighting people, intermediate and advanced portrait methods, and advanced color portraiture. The paths to careers in portraiture vary greatly, but becoming skilled with a camera is essential, whether by learning on the job or by pursuing a degree in photography.

If you're looking for a position in a high-quality professional studio, your portfolio will be the most important asset in winning the job. Studio pros want to know that when they turn a job over to an employee, it will be handled with both creativity and technical perfection.

The studio owner might ask to see contact sheets as well as individual finished prints. The contact sheets show how you take photographs: Do you take many different poses or only a few? Do you try different angles, exposures, lenses, lighting, backgrounds?

School Portrait Photography

Consider that virtually every student from preschool through high school and college is photographed every year, and you begin to see the wealth of possibility in the school portrait business. Schools may need photographs of classroom groups, for student identification cards, for student files, for the yearbook, and of student activities, clubs, dances, and events.

Schools rarely have a photographer on staff, relying instead on any of three types of companies: local studios that contract with the school for all photography needs; chain studios that offer school photography as part of the repertoire; or specialty school photographers who bid on school contracts and send the film to development labs that specialize in school photography. Some companies specialize in class and individual portraits or events such as dances or student productions; others handle all kinds of school photography.

The Workday

A school photographer works during school hours in the months that school is in session. Because the workload isn't constant, photographers are often part-time employees. For individual portraits, the photographer sets up a portable "studio" in the gym or other room at the school. Portrait sessions are scheduled at five- or ten-minute intervals, and the photographer must keep a careful record of which frames were taken of which students.

The film is sent to the development labs, and the photographer selects the frame to be printed. Proofs are made and then distributed to the students for approval, unless "package deals" are ordered in advance, in which case the image is printed in an agreed-upon number and size for distribution to the students.

Usually provision is made for retakes for those who were absent for the first sessions or dissatisfied with their photographs, as well as additional print orders for those who were delighted.

Working with young people, not all of whom want to be photographed, can be challenging. Given the short time allowed for taking each photo, it is important to work efficiently and interact well with people.

Salaried student portrait photographers start at an average of about $15,000 annually. Sometimes sales commissions or other employee benefits enhance the salary. The work also provides valuable experience for the beginning photographer. Although you don't have to have experience to apply, companies are likely to hire those with some photography background.

Chain and Department Store Studios

Working for a chain or department store photography studio is often an excellent place to begin a career as a portrait photographer. In this kind of studio, you see it all—the best and the worst of the business—which allows you to gain experience and sample the work environment before making the investment to strike out as an independent. Often you will be only one of many photographers on staff. In many cases, photographers work with a manager and assistant manager, and their supervisory responsibilities include scheduling enough photographers to cover the long hours, particularly at department stores and malls.

The equipment is standard and fixed, and the major challenge, as with school photography, lies in capturing the expression of the client. Often chain studios are willing to hire students part-time or as interns. Because of the standard equipment setup, people skills are often more important than photography experience. Clients are most often families with children or children alone. The number of photo sessions is high, particularly around holidays. Jobs are plentiful, relatively easy to obtain, and the experience gained can be invaluable.

Independent Portrait Studios

The variety of work situations is greater in independent establishments. Independent studios sometimes send photographers to shoot on location and often shoot weddings or other events. Some studios are small one-person operations; others are minichains in themselves. Sometimes the lab work is done in-house; sometimes it is sent out. Entry-level work can involve everything from sweeping the floors, loading film in the camera, and assisting with photo sessions to general business chores such as phoning clients, processing orders and sales, and keeping records of portrait sittings.

Don't underestimate the value of learning how a small business functions from the ground up. It may provide the impetus and insight you need later to start your own business.

Owning Your Own Studio

For independent types, starting and owning your own portrait studio is a dream that can be made real. Be forewarned: Competition is fierce! A lot of portraiture is done by low-cost regional and national chains in department stores and malls. They offer convenience and, more and more frequently, services such as one-hour portrait development, passport photographs, and photographic restoration. Independent portrait studios do exist and thrive, though, because they can offer a level of quality and personal service that makes them unique.

Before you hang up your shingle and spend a lot of money on studio space, equipment, and advertising, make sure you've got what it takes to make it on your own. Marilyn Sholin sums it up this way: "The prime prerequisite to becoming a professional photographer and to making a living at it is to have the heart and soul of an entrepreneur. Without that you will end up working it just like it's another job and end up 'shooting kids' at JCPenney and Sears."

There are many questions to consider as you plan:

- What are the needs in the community you hope to serve?
- What competition exists in your region?
- Is there something you can offer that will set your studio apart from the others?
- Do you have a network to connect you to people and help get you started?
- Do you have clients who will recommend you?
- Will you advertise?
- What other marketing will you do?
- Do you own enough equipment to get started?
- What equipment will you purchase?
- What about studio space?
- What about storage?
- What about the legal issues of incorporation and licensing in your community?
- Who will handle your accounting?
- Do you need additional capital?
- Can you do it alone?
- Can you support yourself?

Spend some time thinking about the pros and cons of starting your own studio. Your own abilities aren't the only variable to consider. Thoroughly research your locale and the logistics of operating a business. Numerous resources exist for small-business owners. Start with your nearest Small Business Development Center (SBDC), operated through community or junior colleges. The SBDC provides information and assistance on marketing, taxes, accounting, and loan proposals. Depending on the center, available resources may include evening classes, counseling, or a library of books, videos, and computers.

Benefits of Owning Your Own Business

- Being the boss means having the freedom to set your own hours and organizational procedures.
- With the appropriate portable studio equipment, you can work out of your home.

- There's a direct relationship between how much energy you put into your work and how much you earn.
- You can establish a specialty for your studio that relates to an area you're especially interested in.

Things to Consider Before Starting

- You are solely responsible—it won't be as easy to leave your job at the office at the end of the day.
- You'll have to spend time on finances and accounting and marketing—not just working the camera.
- You'll have to make a significant capital investment in equipment, advertising and promotion, and studio facilities.

Advice from Entrepreneurs

Building a client base and starting a business can be incredibly challenging, but extremely rewarding as well. Brian Beauban, owner of Beauban Photography in Berwyn, Illinois, advises that the aspiring studio owner develop "an understanding of sound business practices—marketing, bookkeeping, management skill, and luck." Read books on marketing and salesmanship and seek out local photographers willing to talk about their experiences, he suggests. Study your market. Develop a reputation for good work and ethical business practices. "But most important," Brian says, "is to learn from your mistakes; don't keep tripping over them."

Doing the research first was crucial to the success of Rick Nye, owner of Rick Nye Photography in Orem, Utah. "The best thing I did was to visit all the local studios, study their layouts, get price information, determine where they were lacking and capitalize on it." Rick Nye Photography has grown from a freelance business to a retail store location despite a glut of studios in his small town because, Rick says, "I put a lot of emphasis on creativity and customer service. I firmly believe a studio's atmosphere and treatment of the customer determines whether or not the sale brings in repeat business, not the price structure as most will believe.

"It's a business as well as an art, and you need to be proficient at both! One can't survive without the other."

A Case Study

Marilyn Sholin owns a professional studio, Photography by Marilyn, in North Miami Beach, Florida. Working as a buyer in a major department store gave her a solid retail background in both buying and advertising. Her older brothers were camera nuts who had a basement darkroom. She borrowed a camera, and the first roll of film she shot won a regional Kodak contest for amateurs.

She began her portrait photography career by photographing her sons and taking every photographic course she could find locally. She took portrait photographs for friends of their children and was encouraged to start charging for her work. Working out of her home, Marilyn started to build a client base. She has since operated in several retail locations.

The Pros and Cons. Marilyn stresses the large amount of time spent dealing with the public and coping with varied personalities. "The one thing I can say is that you must like people to be in this business," she advises. That aspect of her work provides her with both delights and challenges. "I would say that my number one reward is becoming part of so many families. I get to watch the babies grow into young men and women and to see the happiness on grandparents' faces. I get to participate in the happy moments in a family's life and put a little piece of myself into their homes for them to enjoy forever."

She also cites the benefits of being her own boss ("although the clients are always dictating the hours") and the creative rewards of trying out her own ideas. "I enjoy watching the perfect expression on a mother's face as she looks at her newborn. When I can paint her with beautiful lighting and put her in a soft setting, the end result can take my breath away."

A Typical Week, a Typical Job. Marilyn's workweek includes meeting with employees to resolve questions, receiving updates from her bookkeeper about unpaid invoices, and answering correspondence, as well as, of course, taking photographs of clients.

One two-hour session she recalls illustrates the humor, demands, and rewards that are constant in portrait photography.

"Eight people arrive for a family portrait with grandparents, parents, children, a dog, and a three-month-old baby. I start with the largest group, and the baby has trouble staying awake. When the baby wakes up, the dog starts barking, and the baby starts crying. Everyone falls out of the pose and tries to calm the dog down. I put everyone back together and check clothing and makeup and get a few good poses done.

"Baby starts crying again. I decide to do some portraits of just the grandparents. While I am doing that, the baby falls asleep again. Baby's two-year-old sister suddenly wants to do pictures right now. I finish the grandparents and go on to do some pictures of the sister alone. Then the grandmother says she won't want those photos without the baby. I tell her I can also photograph the baby alone, and she can put the pictures in a double frame. She says no because it will cost too much. I try now to wake up baby softly and put her in sister's lap.

"I get a few shots done until someone lets go of the dog and he runs into the shot and starts licking the baby's face and makes the baby cry again. I finally get the whole thing settled down, and we get all the portraits done. They are all happy now, and the baby is wide awake and smiling as they put her in the car."

Wedding and Event Photography

Wedding photography is a huge business, both for professional studio photographers and freelancers. Both still photography and videography are commonly used for weddings and events such as bar mitzvahs and bat mitzvahs, first communions, baptisms, graduations, installations, and any other ceremonial functions.

Event photography is more like photojournalism than studio work because there are no second chances to catch the significant or decisive moments. You need to anticipate the action and be in the right place at the right time or the opportunity is lost.

Dealing with the high emotions usually surrounding an event like a wedding can be a challenge as well. Such situations call for exceptional people management skills. Weekend work is a necessity, of course, and the client sets the hours to a necessary degree.

Wedding and event photography can provide some freedom in terms of equipment, approaches, and artistry. As in any business, the freedom gained by freelancing also carries responsibility—you will be judged by your product!

Wedding and event photographers often develop their own prints; however, many custom labs specialize in wedding photography. One freelance wedding photographer advises that "not having full control of the prints is a surefire way to go out of business fast. Never, never, never give the client the negs!"

The Workday

Because most weddings take place on the weekends or in the evening, that's when you do a large part of your work. For this reason, wedding photographers often have a day job or provide the service as an extension of a portrait studio business.

The wedding photographer documents the entire wedding process, sometimes including the rehearsal dinner and bachelor and bachelorette parties. Certainly it involves photographing at the wedding itself, with most formal portraits taken very soon after the ceremony or after guests have passed through the receiving line at the reception. The idea is to photograph the bride and all the attendants—flower girls, ring bearers, parents, grandparents—before the inevitable cake and coffee stains start to appear.

This can be a Herculean task for a photographer working alone, which is why many wedding photographers work with an assistant or draft the services of a young relative at the event. Everyone is understandably excited about the ceremony and busy visiting, so an orderly procession for portraits is a challenge.

A Freelance Wedding Photographer

Laura Benjamin, a freelance photographer since 1986, takes on many wedding jobs. "They are among the best and worst in terms of work conditions," she says. "Emotions run high. It's difficult sometimes to stay calm. Of course I worry about ruining the shoot—the disappointment involved is excruciating to consider. "It's never happened," she adds. "But still, I worry. But it can also be an immensely satisfying role, to be capturing one of the most important events in someone's life. When I get candids that reveal special moments, like the bride's niece throwing rice over her head, laughing, at the reception, I know I've caught a moment that will make people smile."

Sometimes Laura uses an assistant, often a student, to help her. Assistants don't do any of the shooting—they help haul equipment and arrange people for group shots. They stay on the lookout for good photo opportunities. Laura comments about having assistants, "it helps relieve the chaos of some of those long wedding and reception days—and it gives them a great chance to experience this sort of work."

Going Digital

Charles and Jennifer Maring own and operate Maring Photography, Inc., in Wallingford, Connecticut. They've been involved in digital photography for several years, primarily with portraits, but recently they began shooting the majority of their wedding jobs with Nikon D-1 and Nikon D-1X cameras. Charles recommends in a March 2002 *Rangefinder* magazine article that photographers frequently back up their digital images—especially after any change has been made to the image.

Charles makes at least four backups during the processing of wedding photographs. He has also begun to use digital prints for proofing purposes because he can present a bound book of numbered images that the clients can handle and refer to more easily than the old loose proofs.

The cost savings for digital photography have been significant as well. In addition to saving on film and processing expenses, the amount of time saved by being able to download images directly from the camera rather than having to clean dust off film or prints and then scan them into the computer has been significant.

The design aspects of digital photography have also appealed to Charles and Jennifer. Charles notes in particular the layering techniques and design elements that became possible with the advent of programs like Photoshop and Painter.

Starting on Your Own

Since most wedding photography business comes from referrals, getting started can be the most difficult part of the business. A good approach is to start taking photographs for friends as your wedding gift to them. Just handle the experience as if you had been hired as a professional. Those photographs will become your portfolio, and you don't want them to look like snapshots.

For young photographers breaking into the portrait business, Marilyn Sholin suggests getting a job with Glamour Shots, a chain studio across the United States, or with a department store studio operation. "It will give them a chance to work with a lot of people and learn while they earn some money," Marilyn explains. "It also will allow someone else to absorb their beginners' mistakes, and it won't hurt their reputations when they go out on their own."

One tip is to attend local bridal fairs as an exhibitor. Although renting a booth can be expensive, the advertising opportunity can be well worth it. Potential clients will get to see your work, bringing them one step closer to hiring you.

Potential Earnings

A professional private studio charges an average of $100 to $150 for a portrait sitting, with a range of $50 to $300. The sitting includes one eight-by-ten-inch print; then the client places an order for additional prints from an à la carte price list that includes discounts for large orders.

The same studio charges an average of $1,800 for professional wedding services, depending on the number of sessions required. The photographer then prints proof sheets, and the bride, groom, and their family members place orders for prints.

An assistant working for a professional studio starts at between minimum wage and $15 per hour and can earn considerably more as an experienced assistant or associate photographer. An associate is someone who is capable of taking over for the photographer if necessary and generally works with his or her own equipment. A photographer without previous studio or wedding experience might be hired as a trainee and be paid close to minimum wage.

The Video Angle

Some clients will want to have both still photographs and videos taken at the wedding. If you want to keep all the business in-house, you might consider subcontracting the videography or hiring someone to perform these services on staff. See Chapter 13 for more information on videography careers.

Magazine Sales

Some of your best wedding photographs might well be marketable to any of the numerous bridal magazines on the market, as well as to photography magazines. A magazine might pay $150 or more for a color photograph used full page, and up to $2,500 for a cover photograph. Before you can sell a wedding or portrait photograph to a magazine or other publisher, you must receive the client's or model's permission in writing.

Glamour and Boudoir Photography

Glamour photography is primarily, though not exclusively, involved with glamorous portraits of women. This genre may have had its start during the war, when soldiers wanted keepsakes of their sweethearts to carry with them.

Nowadays, these portraits are taken for aspiring models, both male and female, young and old. Would-be models need to have "slicks"—photographs showing them at their most photogenic—to show to agents or prospective employers.

Boudoir photography, as the name implies, involves bedroom pictures. Again, these are mostly, but not always, women in a provocative pose or setting, either nude or scantily clad. The purposes for these photographs vary according to the client: a wife might want to give her husband a special Valentine gift; a young man may be hoping to "audition" for a magazine centerfold.

The boudoir photography market has emerged in part as a result of *Playboy* and *Playgirl* magazines and the growing popularity of intimate apparel catalogs, such as Victoria's Secret.

Working with Models

Seasoned glamour and boudoir photographers advise that beginning photographers have an assistant on hand at all times, preferably the same gender as the client or model. This helps put the client at ease and protects you and the model or client from charges of impropriety.

If you're just getting started and need to build a portfolio, you can often find models who will pose in exchange for their own slicks. If you hope to sell the photographs, you need a model release form signed, giving you permission to use the photographs for specific purposes (see Chapter 7 for more information).

You also need someone who is extremely proficient in makeup, hair styling, and costuming to give your clients the right look. Clients may arrive with no idea how to go about making themselves look glamorous, so you may need to do some "directing." Without expert application of makeup, styling, and wardrobe, the portraits probably won't cross into the realm of "glamour."

You also need to be something of a diplomat, flattering sincerely without pouring on the butter boat. You might need to pose a client to minimize less attractive features or capitalize on good features. Certainly you can emphasize the good, but beware of pointing out the less than perfect.

Potential Earnings

Many glamour and boudoir photographers work solely as portraitists for clients. The photographs are most often made as gifts, and the package price often includes a gift folder. Fees for glamour or boudoir photos are typically higher than for standard portraiture because of the additional attention to makeup and setting.

The market for glamour and boudoir photographs, aside from taking photographs for clients, is primarily for magazines and other printed products, such as calendars. Advertisers, too, look for photographers with a strong glamour portfolio for products ranging from cosmetics to lingerie, cars to travel resorts.

Catalogs, especially those for intimate apparel or swimsuits, are also a good market. Photographers working on assignment for advertisers or magazines can expect to make $350 to $2,150 per day, depending on their experience and reputation. Per-photo sales range from $50 to $1,500, depending on the use. Some paper-products companies pay a percentage of sales earnings (see Chapter 6 for more information).

For More Information

Books

Family Portrait Photography: Professional Techniques & Images, by Helen T. Boursier. Amherst Media.

Fifty Portrait Lighting Techniques for Pictures that Sell, by John Hartl. Watson-Guptill.

Master Posing Guide for Portrait Photographers: A Complete Guide to Posing Singles, Couples and Groups, by J. D. Wacker. Amherst Media.

Photographing People: Portraits, Fashion, Glamour. RotoVision SA.

Portrait Photographer's Handbook, by Bill Hunter. Amherst Media.

Portrait Studio Information Package (compilation of articles on the portrait studio business available from the Photo Marketing Association, updated regularly, www.pmai.org.)

Professional Portraiture, by Annabel Williams. Silver Pixel Press.

Professional Secrets of Natural Light Portrait Photography: Techniques and Images, by Douglas Allen Box. Amherst Media.

The Entrepreneur and Small Business Marketing Problem Solver,
by William A. Cohen. Wiley.
The Joy of Photographing People, by Eastman Kodak Company
staff. Addison-Wesley Longman.

Periodicals

Studio Photography and Design
Cygnus Publishing
P.O. Box 460
Fort Atkinson, WI 53538

WPPI Newsletter
Wedding & Portrait Photographers International
www.wppi-online.com
  (Monthly membership newsletter)

Organizations

Professional Photographers of America
229 Peachtree Street NE, Suite 2200
Atlanta, GA 30303
www.ppa.com

Professional School Photographers Association (PSPA)
  A division of Photo Marketing Association International (PMA)
3000 Picture Place
Jackson, MI 49201
www.pmai.org

Wedding & Portrait Photographers International
1312 Lincoln Boulevard
Santa Monica, CA 90401
www.wppi-online.com

CHAPTER FIVE

The Selling Game

Commercial and Advertising Photography

I f you're interested in combining artistic vision and creativity in your photographs with high income potential, a career in advertising or commercial photography may suit you perfectly. Advertising is probably the highest paying field in photography, and it involves nearly every possible subject matter, from high fashions to farm implements, exotic animals to eggs Benedict.

Allyn Solomon, a photographer's representative in New York City who has worked with some of the top photographers in the business, wrote in his book, *Advertising Photography*, "Advertising photography at its best represents something attractive to the public, not because it 'manipulates' but because it makes us visually aware. . . . In advertising, those with a style, a vision, are hired as photographers . . . much as the artists of the Renaissance were engaged by the Medicis."

Solomon suggests that it is the artists among the commercial photographers who have attained the pinnacle of success in this demanding, high-paced field. A sense of personal style and vision have made their work stand out among others, and advertisers want their products to do the same.

So far, this is an area that is dominated by men. The national figures in the Advertising Professionals of America report in 1999 showed that 85 percent were male, despite a significant increase in the number of women enrolled in photography schools in the previous decade. This gender gap, apparent in all areas of photography, is wider in advertising and commercial photography.

Commercial Photography Growth

The 1950s saw a surge in the growth of advertising in general and in the use of photography in particular. America's growing affluence meant more discretionary income was being spent on a wide variety of goods and services, and it was up to the advertisers to let the public know what was available.

Today, advertising and marketing are part of a complex amalgam of market testing research and psychology as well as artistic vision and creativity. Before a corporation spends millions of dollars on advertising, the executives want to be certain that the "pitch" of the campaign is going to be successful.

The cost of getting information to the public has increased dramatically, and the number of channels for advertising has also expanded—in print and in broadcast media and on the World Wide Web. Cable television companies are competing vigorously with established network and local stations for advertising revenue, and magazines and catalog businesses have expanded their market reach by establishing presence on the Internet.

Virtually every magazine on the newsstand has an editorial-to-advertising ratio that edges closer to fifty-fifty all the time. Recent growth in the mail-order catalog business has boosted opportunities in this field as well. More than fifteen billion mail-order catalogs are sent to homes and businesses each year, accounting for more than $357 billion in annual sales. The central content of those catalogs and promotional materials is photography. The market for advertising and commercial photography has never been larger.

Who Hires Commercial Photographers

Corporations

Major corporations employ large staffs in their advertising departments, including researchers, copywriters, graphic designers, photographers, and art directors. Companies without—and sometimes those with—advertising departments hire advertising agencies, which may or may not have photographers on staff. The art director for a corporation or advertising agency is responsible for hiring photographers to work on various projects. The art director is the liaison between the photographer and the client with the product to be photographed.

Every business, large or small, needs some means of letting the public or potential patrons know about what it offers, whether a product or a service. Most often, this will involve a photographer at some level. The range of photography subjects is as broad as the products and services currently on the market. You might take a series of still-life photos one day, action-oriented shots the next. Your work might take you on location, especially if you work with the fashion or auto industries, where exotic or picturesque settings serve as enticing backdrops to the high-priced products.

The larger the corporation, the better the chance that the advertising staff will include one or more photographers. If there isn't a staff photographer, the advertising art director will review portfolios presented either by photographers themselves or through photo representatives. Even smaller corporations may hire photographers directly to provide executive portraits or grip-and-grin shots to accompany press releases or publicity packets, as well as product photographs for advertising purposes.

Advertising Agencies and Design Studios

Hired by the corporate client, the advertising agency or graphic design studio fulfills the role of the corporate advertising department. A team of advertising professionals together develop the strategy, concepts, and design and layout for the advertising campaign and its components. The design studio becomes involved primarily with design and layout and may be the one to provide photographic services.

Advertising agencies and designers generally develop a "stable" of photographers to provide the images they need, but art directors often review new portfolios for particular projects or to keep tabs on who is available and who is producing what kind of work.

Magazines

From fashion magazines to publications for car buffs, the slick publications on newsstands today are filled with the work of commercial photographers. Since not many magazines have photographers on staff, opportunities abound to join the stable of photographers given top assignments.

Magazine photography encompasses virtually every subject area. If you have developed a subject specialty, you will be in a good position to establish an ongoing relationship with the magazines published for that interest. Chapters 3 and 6 provide additional information on magazine photography.

Public Relations Firms

Public relations (PR) photography is closely related to advertising; in fact, it's often referred to as "free advertising." The goal of PR photography is to make the public feel good about a product or a company. A company sends out a news release about a new product, an award won by the marketing department, a new development by the research department, or a new CEO ready to take the reins of the organization. The press release is often accompanied by photographs for the newspaper or trade magazine to use.

A PR photographer is involved with a variety of subjects, from product photography to portrait photography. PR photographers also have a close relationship to photojournalists because the photographs they take are generally intended for publication as part of a news article.

Retail Stores and Mail-Order Catalogs

I combine these categories because often a retailer that is large enough to advertise and need the services of a photographer also produces its own catalog. This is a good area for photographers beginning in the industry to get an introduction to fashion photography because of the large number of clothing catalogs—from the status-oriented Nieman Marcus to the down-home look of L.L. Bean, from Bloomingdale's to JCPenney. Department store photographers might shoot products, window displays, events such as fashion shows, and public relations photos. A department store photographer might also set up a Polaroid camera production for photographs with a store Santa.

Furniture stores often produce mail-order catalogs, which involves staging and shooting interiors. A photographer who has strong experience with interiors might also work for interior decorators or architects, or for magazines such as *House & Garden, Home,* or *Architectural Digest.*

Government: Tourism and Economic Development Departments

State and city governments often have a need to advertise in order to attract tourists or businesses interested in investing in the local economy. Departments of tourism or economic development often produce colorful, descriptive pamphlets or brochures and sometimes develop advertising campaigns that feature beautiful photographs of the region, its architecture or scenic attractions, and its people. A photographer might work directly with the project manager or with an advertising agency hired to produce the promotional piece.

Colleges and Universities

The competition for students among the nation's colleges and universities, both public and private, involves the development of catalogs and brochures that are becoming increasingly sophisticated in both content and quality. In striving for quality, the art director or designer will most likely want the services of a professional commercial photographer, one who knows how to shoot for product appeal. The product, in this case, involves the campus itself and its students, faculty, research and creative endeavors, sports, and any other aspect of college or university life.

The Entertainment Industry

Although we think of movie camera operations when we think of the television and film industry, still photographers are much in demand in this business. A still photographer working for Turner

Broadcasting, for example, would be involved with taking publicity stills of shows in production, portrait shots of star actors, stage shots, or other promotional product shots.

In Hollywood, too, photographers on the back lot are a common part of the scene. They capture still shots on location, behind-the-scenes shots for public relations purposes, and posed photographs for both trade and fan publications.

Performing Arts Organizations

Theaters, especially, require the services of photographers in preparing production stills for advertising purposes. Symphony orchestras, opera companies, ballet corps, and modern dance troupes all require specialized photography for promotions, advertising specific performances, showcasing big-name talent, and fund-raising publications.

Performing arts photography is generally done during a full dress rehearsal, a "photo call" arranged specifically for the purpose of taking photographs, or on opening night. Major concert or performance houses that present traveling productions may have a photographer on staff to handle local publicity needs.

Photographs taken during musical performances have other potential markets. Local newspapers and magazines, trade publications for arts professionals, and record companies all buy performance photos.

Record Companies

From shooting album covers in the studio to rock concerts in the coliseum, the commercial photographer who works for record companies has many professional opportunities and great earning potential. Like fashion and entertainment, the record industry is one in which a photographer can earn a measure of fame, as well as good money. But that takes years of hard work and experience.

In order to get started earning that experience, newcomers to the field often approach smaller, independent record companies. Larger companies generally have several freelance or staff photographers they work with regularly.

Genres in Advertising Photography

Fashion Photography

This is the glamour trade, the world of high fashion. Photographers at the top in this industry are earning big money, gaining fame and prestige, and living a glamorous life filled with beautiful people in beautiful places wearing beautiful clothes.

Richard Avedon is perhaps the guru of this genre. Although Avedon is not just a fashion photographer, he is largely responsible for the status of the craft today. Most photographers don't aspire to such heights, but a lot can be learned about the genre by studying the works of Avedon, Beaton, Horst, Scavullo, and others whose names are household words among photography's elite.

Fashion photographers work in all corners of the country, from department store fashion shows to the new fall announcements in New York. Fashion is an area that offers international opportunities because so much of the high-fashion world is centered in Europe—primarily in Paris, Milan, and London.

Garment manufacturers, clothing stores, mail-order catalog merchants, magazine publishers, and modeling agencies are all potential customers of the fashion photographer.

Food Photography

According to one professional photographer, food is where the money is, not necessarily because the day rate is higher here than in other areas of advertising, but because there are so many different food-related companies needing your services. It's not too difficult to keep busy—if you're good.

Food is one of the most difficult advertising subjects to master. It takes a special skill to make your photograph so powerful that the viewer salivates just looking at it. Some photographers rely on oils, resins, and other tricks to make the product look appetizing. Others prefer to capture that "fresh from the oven" presentation. Composition, lighting, and design are the dominant considerations in food photography.

Dana Marks is a still-life photographer who specializes in food. Her clients include cooking magazines and several New York restaurants and food products corporations. Her studio has a separate kitchen with three restaurant-sized ovens, a walk-in freezer, and two refrigerators. Her staff includes a cook, a food stylist who scours stores for the perfect strawberry or a set of flatware in a style that complements the still life, a lighting technician, and a general assistant who helps with everything from labeling film and keeping photo session logs to rushing food hot from the kitchen.

Food photographers work for magazines, food growers and packagers, appliance manufacturers, restaurants, and industry trade associations.

Product Photography

Although food and fashion are considered products, the genre of product photography involves broader technical expertise that allows a photographer to take on virtually any product challenge, from photographing a new Boeing 747 to shooting a package of sewing needles.

Lighting, composition, background, color, texture, scale—all the elements of art and design—come into play when taking product photographs. Commercial product photographers are often darkroom or Photoshop magicians, creating special concoctions with chemicals or digital filters to achieve the right effects.

The product photographer working for advertising purposes needs to have an artist's vision in order to set up still lifes of a product that can entice the viewer into buying. Another aspect of the product photographer's work involves strict documentation of a product for purposes of identification or trademark registration.

Photo Illustration

An illustrator is someone who creates a visual "story" to accompany written text. A photo illustrator does the same thing but uses photography rather than pastels and paints.

Photo illustration is used by any of the clients described earlier in this chapter, primarily for purposes of advertising and promotions. Magazines and newspapers also use photo illustration to illustrate articles. Book publishers are also potential clients.

With digital technology, photo illustrators often combine photographic talent with computerized manipulation. Andy Baird, author of *The Macintosh Dictionary* and prototyper of multimedia educational software, captures still images using computer software to scan through the video film images until he finds the perfect combination.

"One of the best things about this style of work," Andy says, "is that unlike a still camera, with videotape there's no fear of missing the 'decisive moment' because you can replay a scene over and over until you manage to hit the 'Grab Frame' button at just the right instant. Add Photoshop and a Wacom tablet with pressure-sensitive stylus, and you have the makings of some real fun!"

What It Takes

Commercial and advertising photographers need to have technical expertise down cold. Handling lighting, cameras, formats, and film needs to be second nature. There is no room for error when a client is paying you $2,500 per day to shoot beautifully lit, perfectly proportioned, aesthetically composed photographs of a product—whether it's a bowl of cereal or an expensive objet d'art.

Original Style

With technical expertise as a given, the highly successful advertising photographer also has a certain flair or style that's unique, not a pale imitation of someone else's. Get to know the work of the major photographers in the field; look closely at all kinds of advertising photography and analyze the styles you see.

Your own style is developed over time through experimentation, trial, and error. What is more important initially is that you bring your creativity and collaboration in the effort to capture the viewer's attention and hold it long enough for the message to come across. An art director reviewing your portfolio will be looking for both technical ability and aesthetic vision.

Special Expertise

As you gain experience, you might want to begin to specialize, to create a niche for your work so your name is the one art directors think of when they have a project that fits your specialty. Specialty areas in commercial and advertising photography include still life (food, retail, product, catalog, and editorial) and people photography (fashion, beauty or glamour, portraiture, lifestyle, sports/fitness, and corporate). According to the Advertising Photographers of America, product photography accounts for one-fifth of all commercial photography, with corporate and lifestyle advertising close behind, each with 12 percent of the total. Other specialties include architecture, automotive, concept illustration, and music/entertainment.

There may well be crossover categories in commercial and advertising photography. For example, you may be photographing potato chips both as part of a still life and within a setting of people enjoying the product. Or an advertisement for shampoo becomes part still life and part beauty or glamour photo. When you're just developing your portfolio, you will probably want to include several representations for each of several categories or specialties. Follow Allyn Solomon's advice: "Shoot to eat, but don't lose sight of the need always to heed the development of your style. This is the key to creative survival."

Knowledge of Printing and Technology

Understanding what the printing process demands of photography is an important skill to offer an advertising client. For example, knowing whether the images will be "ganged"—grouped together for color separation, one of the more costly elements of color printing production—will make a great deal of difference in how you shoot a series of products for a catalog producer.

It's important for the photographer to come to a job with this information; otherwise, when the project gets bogged down in production, the client will come back unhappy that your lack of understanding is going to mean higher printing costs on the final product. The best way to gather this information is to work closely with the designer and production people who will be working with your photographs.

The digital revolution has made a huge impact in commercial and advertising photography, although most advertising photographers still shoot with film. Images are then digitized using scanners or expensive camera backs that translate the film data to the computer directly. Expertise with Photoshop software is more important in the advertising industry than perhaps any other because of the need to maximize the image's potential and often to create multilayered photo illustrations of products.

Business Savvy

A good business sense is also important for a commercial photographer working independently. You need to be willing to market yourself or work with a good rep who will present your portfolio to art directors, schedule your projects, and negotiate your fees. Those photographers who have the sharpest business skills and an aptitude for marketing themselves and their services will have the greatest success as independent studio owners.

People Skills

Depending on the situation, you may have photographers' assistants, models, stylists, food preparation specialists, designers, and art directors to deal with in the course of a photo session. You need to work both as a director of people and as a photographer. In addition, independent commercial photographers need to be able to work with clients, discovering their preferences and prejudices, encouraging a more creative or effective solution, or simply maintaining a good business relationship.

Equipment

The investment in equipment for a professional commercial photographer can be staggering. The Advertising Photographers of America survey revealed that, on average, respondents had more than $130,000 invested in cameras and lighting, darkroom, digital imaging, and office equipment. Medium- and large-format (four-by-fives and eight-by-tens) and 35 mm cameras are the most commonly used. Nearly 95 percent of the photographers surveyed use a computer for business, and of those, the majority use Macs.

....

Getting Started

As with most other areas of photography, one of the best ways to get the training you need—aside from attending college and earning a bachelor's or associate's degree in photography—is to begin by working as a photo assistant for an established professional. While you're in school, take advantage of every possible opportunity for honing your skills as a photographer. Obtain an internship with a photographer or studio that specializes in a subject matter that interests you. Start to develop your own creative style. Experiment with genres and techniques. Develop a portfolio to show potential clients. Resign yourself to starting small—as a photo assistant or apprentice. It's difficult to obtain that first job in this competitive business, or even to start out on your own.

Photo Reps

Of the photographers surveyed by the Advertising Photographers of America, 40 percent had reps who handled marketing and fee negotiations for a commission. The average commission paid on a job is 24 percent, although usually the rep's fee is added to what the photographer hopes to receive rather than deducted from that amount.

....

Income Potential

Salaried employees just starting out in commercial or advertising photography will likely earn $14,950 to $35,000 per year. That figure will rise to $31,400 to $102,000 or more with experience and depending on the specific field of commercial photography. High-fashion photography is the most lucrative.

An independent photographer operating a commercial studio can earn up to $200,000 per year, especially in the areas of corporate photography and catalog photography. But these figures imply the photographer is someone with excellent business savvy, as well as photographic skills, creativity, and a solid reputation.

Freelancers in commercial photography can earn from $300 to $2,500 per day for their services, or they can sell individual photographs for $50 to $4,000, depending on how the images are used. The rates vary by photographic subject, client, and geographic location. Fashion and entertainment photographers earn more than, say, photo illustrators; advertising agencies pay more than public relations agencies; and New York, Chicago, and Los Angeles continue to be more lucrative markets in commercial photography than other cities.

Advertising and commercial photographers earn about 10 percent of their incomes from stock usage fees. When completing a photo shoot, the photographer transfers one-time-use rights to the client for the purpose of publishing a brochure, catalog, advertisement, or package. If the client wants to re-use that photo—or if another client wants to use it—then the photographer charges fees ranging from $100 to $4,500 or more. Single-image fees are lowest for regional catalogs—averaging $180 per image—and climb to an average of $5,200 for photographs used on national billboards.

For More Information

Organizations
Advertising Photographers of America
National Office
145 South Olive Street
Orange, CA 92866
www.apanational.org

Periodicals

Advertising Age
711 Third Avenue
New York, NY 10017
   (Weekly advertising and marketing publication.)

Adweek Agency Directory
Billboard Publications Incorporated
770 Broadway
New York, NY 10003
   (Weekly advertising and marketing magazine.)

Photo District News
Billboard Publications Incorporated
770 Broadway
New York, NY 10003
   (Monthly trade magazine for the photography industry.)

Print: America's Graphic Design Magazine
3200 Tower Oaks Boulevard
Rockville, MD 20852
   (Bimonthly magazine on creative trends in design, illustration, and photography.)

Books and Directories

Professional Photographic Illustration, by Eastman Kodak
   Company staff. Tiffen Company LLC.
Directory of Mail Order Catalogs, by Richard Gottlieb. Grey
   House Publishing.
The Design Firm Management & Administration Report Yearbook,
   by Stephen Kliment et al. IOMA Institute of Management and
   Administration.
*The Fashion & Print 2002 Directory: The Madison Avenue
   Handbook,* by Gregory James et al. Peter Glenn Publications.

CHAPTER SIX

The Independent Shutterbug

Freelance Photography

S ome of the most enjoyable aspects of freelancing are the day-to-day variety, the ability to set your own hours and fees (as negotiated with clients, that is), and the freedom to do the kind of work you love. More than half of all professional photographers work independently, according to the *Occupational Outlook Handbook.* Freelance photography offers opportunities in virtually all the categories presented in this book. A freelancer might work at a wedding on Sunday, shoot glamour portraits on Monday morning and a Little League game in the afternoon, work on a corporate advertising assignment on Tuesday, and sell a series of photos to the newspaper on Wednesday. Thursday the fine art gallery exhibit opening reveals more creative work, and Friday the local auto racing club wants group photos and action shots of the rally. Saturday means hiking along a new nature trail for a travel magazine assignment.

Wait a minute! When does the freelancer get a day off? Well, the work schedule, too, is up to you. You can work as much or as little as you like—or have time and energy for. But as a freelancer, when a job comes up, it's tough to say no.

Freelancing represents an ideal way to break into a career in photography. While keeping the day job for the sake of security, you can freelance evenings and weekends to build your portfolio before making the break to full-time freelancing.

Many independent photographers, in the interest of efficiency, specialize in a given field so that their self-marketing energies are spent getting well known by the editors or buyers in that area. The better known you are, the more work comes your way.

The Publishing World

We're living in the "Information Age" of global communications and technological revolutions, yet the high-tech world of computers hasn't derailed the continuing growth of printed publications—more magazines, books, and newspapers are published today than ever before. Many of these have developed a presence on the Internet, but this is more a supplement to the printed piece rather than a replacement. Some publications exist only on the Internet—E-zines are a growing phenomenon in all areas of interest. Photographs are a staple ingredient in publications, whether in print or online, and freelancers are responsible for a great many of those photos.

Freelancing for Magazines

More than twenty thousand magazines are published in the United States alone, and that number fluctuates month to month as new magazines start publishing and unsuccessful ones fold. Few magazines have photography staff positions beyond the photo editor. A glance through *Photographer's Market*, which lists some six hundred magazines, reveals that many magazines use freelancers to supply more than half and sometimes all of the photos appearing in the editorial content of the magazine.

Magazines can be broken into categories by the audience for which they are intended: the general consumer, the special interest association reader, and the trade reader. Newsmagazines, part of the general consumer market, are covered in Chapter 3.

Consumer Magazines. For many photographers, the beautiful, exotic photographs that leap from the pages of magazines like

National Geographic or *Travel & Leisure* evoke visions of becoming a globe-trotting photographer with an expense account. A dream? Yes, but one that can come true—though not overnight. Breaking into the consumer magazine market, which covers most of the magazines you'll find on the newsstands and more, takes perseverance, marketing strategy, and, of course, great photos that meet the magazine's publishing needs.

"First, I look for the photos I need," says R. B. Stevens, photo editor of *Time* magazine. "Second, I buy the photos I like."

Photo editors at major magazines receive far more submissions in a month than they can possibly print in a year, so your work needs to stand out to be noticed. One photo editor for another major magazine warns freelancers to study the magazine's content. He gets annoyed with photographers who send submissions that are clearly inappropriate for his publication. Submissions also need to fit the magazine's publishing style and content.

Smaller magazines, such as regional or local magazines or those with a targeted audience—gardeners, computer buffs, outdoor sports enthusiasts, or animal lovers, for example—also fit into the general consumer category. These publications might offer more opportunities for the beginning photographer than the larger-circulation magazines.

Special-Interest Publications. National and regional organizations usually need a means of communicating with their members throughout the country, and a magazine or newsletter is often the chosen format. The largest of these association-based publications is *Modern Maturity*, the official publication of AARP (American Association of Retired Persons), which is distributed to anyone over fifty years old in the United States who pays a modest membership fee. It's actually the largest-circulation magazine in the country. Several regional groups within the Automobile Association of America also produce slick magazines, which together have a circulation of more than three million AAA members nationwide.

Special-interest publications offer good opportunities for free-lancers because many are not large enough to hire staff photographers. They do, however, frequently rely on stock photos to supplement the work done by freelancers on assignment or the work of freelancers who submit photos directly for consideration. Financial rewards are generally smaller with the smaller publications, but beginners should consider the tear sheets as part of the pay package.

Trade Publications. Like special-interest magazines, trade publications are directed toward a very specifically defined audience. Some trade publications facilitate communication among members of a given profession or trade, such as *Firehouse Magazine* for firefighters or *Food Distribution Magazine* for executives in the food industry. Trade publications, such as computer or in-flight magazines, also communicate to consumers of a given trade area.

Many of these publications use stock photos because their budgets tend to be more limited than either the special-interest or consumer magazines. The editors and photo editors for these publications are often experts in the profession or trade. It is also important that the photographer's work demonstrate an understanding of and appreciation for the particular subject matter of the trade publication.

Presenting Ideas. The ideal situation for a freelancer is to have several magazines for which to do work fairly consistently. It takes time to establish this sort of relationship with a magazine. The first step is getting someone to look seriously at your work and consider you for an assignment.

One of the most surefire ways to get an assignment is to present an editor with a great idea for an article with the promise of great photos to accompany it. Magazines come out every month, sometimes twice a month or even weekly. The editors are always looking for fresh ideas and viewpoints. If your idea is a winner and your portfolio shows some talent, you'll probably get the job.

Coming up with story ideas, though, means that someone has to do the writing. If you can combine writing skills with your photography, you become a very attractive bargain to editors.

Before you approach a magazine with an idea, do your homework. Thoroughly familiarize yourself with the content of the magazine. What kinds of stories does it publish? What kinds of photos? Does the subject matter fit with your interests? Is the pay scale worth the trouble? You'll find information about what a magazine pays freelancers in the annual *Photographer's Market*. Not all magazines are listed, though, so you may need to request submission guidelines directly from the magazine.

Once you've had one assignment, don't rest on your laurels. Come back with more good ideas. Send a photo postcard with a note to keep your name in the editor's mind. If you make too many phone calls, though, you'll be considered a pest. It's a fine line to walk between persistence and pushiness.

Reselling Photographs. You've completed your assignment. Two or three of the hundreds of photographs you took have been published. Is that it? Do the other shots have to languish in some musty file cabinet in your darkroom? Not if you're enterprising enough to think of other potential clients who might be interested in the same subject matter.

"When I'm out on assignment, I'm always looking for opportunities for more general shots that could be sold to a variety of clients," says Tanya Greeley, a freelance photographer in Seattle, Washington, who works as an occasional stringer for the local daily newspaper. She also assists a local portrait studio with location shoots and regularly pitches ideas to several area magazines.

"Last year I was shooting for a *Times* article for the homes section about the jump in real estate prices on the Sound. I was working with a real estate agent who'd just made a million-dollar home sale on Orcas Island. We were on the ferry, outside because it was an unusually gorgeous day, and I saw the unmistakable dorsal fin of a killer whale, an orca. That gave me time to switch lenses—I always carry my full kit with me, even though the assignment would require limited equipment—and watch it for an opportunity. I couldn't believe my luck. It had disappeared for a while, so I was scanning the water, when it came almost completely out of the water in a perfect arc. You would have thought it was performing for an audience. I sold that shot to the newspaper, then I turned around and sold it to *Sea Kayaker* magazine for $100, to *Sea Magazine* for $150, a greeting card and catalog company for another $250, and a local advertising agency that was working on a state tourism brochure for $350. That's an $850 bonus for a job that I was already getting paid on assignment for. Not bad!"

Of course, those extra sales meant some extra legwork. It meant writing letters and making phone calls to a number of potential buyers before making the final sales. "In all, I'd say I spent about two hours making the extra sales," Tanya adds. "It was well worth it, and now I've made some new contacts for possible future work with the ad agency and two magazines I hadn't worked for before."

What It Pays. Magazines usually have established rates for paying freelancers, and until you've made yourself indispensable, keep the negotiating to a minimum. The rates vary tremendously from one publication to the next. Pay is generally per photo, per assignment, or per day.

Day rates for magazines vary widely. Some will pay $400 a day plus expenses, while others will negotiate a flat fee for a specific number of photos—regardless of how long the job took to shoot. You'll need to decide for yourself what your time is worth, but be careful not to undervalue yourself. "Cut-rate" photographers in the end only see their own profits being undermined as someone else comes along and undercuts the competition. Do ask if expenses are covered for film and processing, as well as any travel costs involved with the assignment.

Per-photo prices range from $10 to more than $1,500, depending on some fairly complex variables, including the photo's expected use, the circulation of the magazine, the size the photo will be published in, and whether the photo will be on the magazine's cover. *Photographer's Market* includes information about the range of payment for individual photographs with each of the magazine listings.

The American Society of Media Photographers publishes a directory of members, called the *ASMP Silverbook,* which includes advertisements of photographers with full-color photographs. This book is used by photo editors at magazines, advertising agencies, and design studios to help locate photographers for assignment work.

Freelancing for Newspapers

Many newspapers, especially statewide dailies and Sunday editions, use freelance photographers. A freelancer in another city or state can cover a local event more easily and cost efficiently than a staff photographer from the newspaper's hometown.

New Is News. Timeliness and newsworthiness are the watchwords in the news media. Did it happen today? Get it in the paper. Did it happen last week? It's old news. Don't bother unless there's some new angle that makes the story interesting all over again.

A "breaking" news event is of special interest to newspapers. If you happen upon something newsworthy—a fire or accident scene, a celebrity event, an arrest (always be careful to stay out of the way of officials)—cover it from as many news angles as possible, then race the film to the newspaper to make the sale.

The question of timeliness means that the freelancer might also need to have access to sophisticated wire or electronic transfer media so that the newspaper can receive photos for rapid deadline processing. Chapter 3 discusses photojournalism and press photography in more detail.

What It Pays. Newspapers generally have staff photographers and so don't rely as heavily on freelancers as do magazines. Also, the budget for freelance photography isn't as generous, so the earning potential is not as high. Although it is difficult to make a living as a full-time newspaper stringer, especially if you are only working for one paper at a time, it can be a good way to get started toward a career either as a freelancer or as a photojournalist.

Day rates for newspapers vary from a very low $45 (essentially minimum wage, which might be offered to a raw beginner) to $500 and vary significantly by geographic region. More often, though, a newspaper pays by the assignment or by the number of photographs published. This rate will vary, too, from $8 for a black-and-white photograph in a small weekly to $1,000 for a color photo on the cover of *Observer Life Magazine.*

Freelancing for Book Publishers

The book publishing industry has been undergoing a tremendous period of change in the past two decades. Megamergers, consolidations, and buyouts have shifted the corporate structure within the book publishing world. The economy of the late 1980s and early 1990s deeply affected the book industry, and it never fully recovered with the late-1990s boom. As a result, budgets are much tighter, and editors are thinking twice about whether they can afford to hire photographers for specific needs or whether to save money and buy stock photos.

Before you send a publisher your portfolio, discover the name of the art director or editor who makes photography decisions. It's always best to submit your work to the person with the power to make the decision. Packages marked simply "Editor" without a specific name get shuffled into a pile that will await review first by an assistant before being passed to the person in charge.

Check with the editor, or the listings in *Photographer's Market,* to learn the preferred method for photographers to submit portfolios. Some publishers will prefer to receive a query letter with a resume of credits and a list of the photographs you have in your "stock." (Stock photography is covered later in this chapter.)

The best deal for photographers in the general book industry is to have a photo used on the cover of a book because it both pays more and achieves wider recognition. As with magazine publishing, payment varies according to how the photograph is used, how large it is reproduced, and whether it's in black and white or color. Rates range dramatically, from $25 to $3,000 for a cover photo, although big fees are rare. Some publishers hire freelancers by the project or by the day, with day rates from $250 to $2,000.

Freelancing for Tabloids, Newsletters, and Other Small Publishers

Several specialty publications are too small to be called magazines and too infrequent to be called newspapers. They often carry the banner title of *newsletter* or *monthly*. These small-budget publications usually have so few staff members that a photographer isn't among them. Most small communities have organizations that publish limited-circulation, tabloid-sized newspapers. They are published weekly, monthly, or sometimes quarterly, and almost all of them include photographs.

The approach to getting freelance work with these publications is not unlike that for magazines or newspapers. Find out what they publish and what the editors are looking for, then present yourself with your portfolio and your ideas.

The potential remuneration, almost always on a per-photo rate, is lowest here, but for that reason the opportunity to be published is often the best. Prices vary from $10 to $50 per photo, but when you're just starting out, the photo credit and line on the resume can be as valuable as the paycheck.

Selling to Postcard and Calendar Publishers

Companies that produce greeting cards, calendars, and posters are often willing to pay top dollar for a photograph that meets a specific need or that appeals to a targeted buying audience. *Photographer's Market* lists more than sixty such companies, with information on the pay scale and how freelancers should submit work. Some prefer stock lists with a query letter, some prefer color contact sheets, and others want to see a complete portfolio.

Photographs of nature and wildlife, nostalgia, seasonal images, scenics, children, humor, and inspirational images are the mainstays of this market. Be sure to know the needs of the company before you send your work, though. One company might want only photographs of children, while another may not want to see any such photographs.

Calendar and card photos can earn from $10 to $800 or more. Some companies offer a royalty percentage of sales revenue, but be sure to ask for an "advance" against royalties, paid upon acceptance, and determine what you will receive from the publisher in the nature of sales reports.

The Corporate World

Advertising and Commercial Photography

Most of the magazines and newspapers in the nation earn far more profits from the advertising revenue they receive than from subscriptions. Look at the advertising you see in the publications you encounter every day. They're filled with photographs, and many of those were taken by freelancers.

Advertising photography can be the most lucrative in the field. Day rates can range up to $3,000 for photographers whose portfolios justify such confidence; however, the higher the income, the higher the expectations. Before you reach too high, be sure you can follow through. This extremely demanding and competitive field covers a broad range of talent and client budget levels. *Photographer's Market* lists more than two hundred firms that hire freelancers—day rates vary from $50 to $2,500—or buy photos outright—at per-image rates from $75 to $5,000.

The key to making it in this area is establishing connections with those who provide the major buyers of advertising space—manufacturers, producers, restaurants, entertainment establishments, hotels, service industry operators—with the creative product that appears in the print media:

- Advertising agencies
- Advertising and design departments of major corporations
- Commercial printers
- Design studios/desktop publishers

On a smaller scale, any business or organization with a service or product to sell needs photography. It's your job to convince these businesses of that need! This is where your marketing skills come in handy. Many small local businesses may not realize the value in producing quality advertising materials or brochures to enhance their sales and profitability. Once you've helped one business prepare promotional advertising materials, you've begun to develop the portfolio that will help you get your next job.

Corporate and Industrial Photography

Corporate and industrial photography is another area with tremendous income potential, one that sees a lot of competition at the upper levels of the pay scale. Someone breaking into the corporate market has a stronger chance with local companies, although it's not impossible to develop national clients.

Corporate and industrial photography involves taking photographs that reflect the role, product, people, service, or image of a corporation. Corporate photography might involve documenting a company meeting or event, such as the company picnic. Portraits of newly hired executives or the employee of the month might be commissioned to be sent with press releases to industry trade publications.

Manufacturers often exhibit their products at trade shows and require strong, colorful photographs for the display area. Slide shows for these events or for employee training are other possibilities for industrial photography.

Any business that offers stock on the public market must by law produce an annual report. In recent years, annual reports have become slick, high-cost documents that serve more as promotional literature than as reports to shareholders. The freelancer starting out might very well get an assignment to do annual report photography for a smaller company or organization. This is a big first step toward success in this area.

Other Corporate Freelance Opportunities

Some other opportunities in the world of business include working with companies that exist in nearly every community. Although many of the following organizations often try to have a staff worker take snapshots, your job is to persuade them that a professional touch is needed to truly meet their objectives.

- **Real estate companies.** Larger real estate agencies print weekly or monthly tabloid advertisers with photographs of the houses listed for sale.
- **Architects, building contractors, and interior and landscape designers.** Professionals in the construction industry frequently need photographs of their projects, from the design phase through final construction and decoration.
- **Insurance agencies.** Insurance agencies often recommend that clients have valuables photographed for insurance records.
- **Lawyers.** Litigation can involve the need for documentation or evidence photography.
- **Artists, museums, and art galleries.** A photographer with a strong understanding of lighting can be very effective at taking photographs of fine art objects.
- **Performing arts organizations.** Theater companies, ballet and dance troupes, symphony orchestras, and opera houses all need to photograph performers, both in performance and individually, for advertising and promotion materials.
- **Business or organization conventions.** Working at conventions to provide photographs of display booths or executives in attendance can be a profitable short-term time investment.

- **Manufacturing companies.** Products need to be photographed for advertising, catalogs, or trade shows.
- **Restaurants.** Photographs of food, the chef, or patrons enjoying the restaurant's atmosphere can enhance a restaurant's advertising efforts.
- **Hotels, motels, and resorts.** Most inns and resorts prepare a variety of self-promotional pieces, from brochures to flyers to pamphlets.
- **Department stores.** Special promotional events, window displays, sale flyers, or fashion shows are all opportunities for the freelance photographer.

People Photography

Working with people can be one of the most enjoyable—and the most trying—aspects of photography. Chapter 4 discusses the role of the commercial portrait studio photographer, but freelancers can find opportunities to photograph people without maintaining an expensive studio.

If you lack experience, begin by working with friends and relatives, treating them as professionally as if they were paying clients. The work you produce can become examples you show to prospective clients.

Generally the freelancer establishes a price for creating the photograph, then offers additional prints at a separate rate. Be careful to respect the going rate. As a beginner, it's reasonable to charge less than the current standard because the client is taking more of a gamble hiring you to complete the work rather than a studio photographer with an established reputation. When you become more confident, however, you will want to charge what your time and talent are worth. There is a wide range of options:

- **Portraits.** Many people prefer to be photographed in their homes or a natural outdoor setting, which makes this an ideal way for the freelancer to get started in this lucrative field.

- **Glamour portraits/boudoir.** Aspiring models need to develop their portfolios for presentation to potential clients.
- **Bar/bat mitzvahs or first communions.** Many families want to document these momentous occasions with photographs of the children or formal portraits at the synagogue or church.
- **Graduations.** High schools, colleges and universities, and sometimes elementary and middle schools hold formal graduation ceremonies that provide ideal opportunities for photographers.
- **Proms.** Many high schools holding proms contract with photographers to photograph couples in a staged setting. Other formal dances during the year offer opportunities.
- **Weddings.** Although highly seasonal, concentrated during the summer months, weddings happen year-round.
- **Sports events.** Every community has some kind of sports event, whether it's intramural volleyball, Little League baseball, elementary school soccer, or community team softball. Photograph the team, take action shots to sell to the newspaper, or shoot individual portraits.
- **Special schools.** Ballet or dance schools, theater programs for children, gymnastics schools and the like all provide wonderful opportunities for the freelancer. Most of these schools work toward a recital or performance. Your photographs will help parents treasure the moments for a lifetime. Elementary schools bring in photographers to provide class and individual portraits. This requires a special portable portrait setup, but the investment can pay off if you obtain enough contracts to cover the expense.
- **Passport photos.** A special dual-shot camera, which provides two identical images on the film, or a medium-format camera is all you need to begin taking passport photographs. You can offer a portable service or establish a relationship with a local department store or other business where you make yourself available to take passport photographs at specified times.

- **Clubs, associations, and organizations.** The local garden club's annual rose show, the booster club's summer carnival, and the senior center's "Pensioner's Prom" are examples of events that provide freelance opportunities for a photographer. Photograph individual members, officers, or the entire membership. College towns have fraternities and sororities that sponsor dances, outings, and other events that can be documented with photography.

Stock Photography

Photographers who have been working at the craft for a long time and have developed their own extensive photo libraries might consider developing a client base that could include other stock agencies as well as the usual clients for stock photography: advertising agencies, book publishers, magazine publishers, corporate advertising departments, travel companies, resorts, the entertainment industry—in short, anyone who uses photography in the course of doing business.

Some photographers manage to make a significant portion of their incomes from selling and reselling photographs through stock photo agencies. Stock agencies are like photo libraries or rental companies that maintain an inventory of thousands of photographs covering a wide range of subjects. Clients pay a fee to use a photograph for a magazine article, corporate brochure, annual report, or catalog. The rate paid depends on the rights being purchased and the final use of the image. One particular stock agency lists prices that vary from $225 for a quarter-page image in a U.S. consumer magazine with a circulation of less than one hundred thousand to $4,000 for a cover photograph on a press run of four million or more. Photographs to be used on the Web range in price from $187 for an icon on a secondary page for a small regional corporation to $2,435 for a full-screen homepage image used by a multinational corporation.

The whole stock photography industry has undergone a sea change with the advent of the Internet and digital technology and the burgeoning of the royalty-free photography business. Royalty-free agencies allow the purchase of photographic images for virtually unlimited use at prices as low as $30 or $40 per image, which has seriously affected the ability of traditional stock agencies to hang onto their market shares. Traditional stock sales account for more than $750 million annually, but royalty-free sales have exceeded $100 million annually, and some predict this could grow to nearly $1 billion in the near future.

The difficulty in making a success of stock photo sales is in marketing and distribution, which is why a relationship with a stock agency is beneficial. You can set up your own stock website, but if you plug the keywords stock photography into any search engine, you'll end up with hundreds of individual photographers' sites to wade through—something a busy photo buyer is unlikely to do.

What Sells in the Stock Market

For a photograph to do well in the photography stock market, it needs to communicate, it needs to be impressive in terms of its technical perfection as well as aesthetic presentation, and it needs to be general rather than specific. You need to be able to envision a hundred different ways for the photograph to be used in order for it to sell to a variety of clients.

Stock agencies often specialize in a given subject matter or several somewhat related subjects. If you've developed a specialty in your own work, you will most likely be able to find a stock photo agency that fits your interests. The very large agencies cover everything and often hire photographers to go out and shoot photos to fill in the gaps in their ability to meet potential client needs.

Categories covered in stock libraries include the following:

- Agriculture
- Architecture
- Armed forces
- Arts and entertainment
- Business

- Celebrities
- Children
- Fashion
- Fine art and crafts
- Food
- Health and fitness
- Hospitals and medicine
- Industry
- Landmarks and landscapes
- Nature
- People
- Planes, trains, and automobiles
- Plants and botany
- Real estate
- Recreation
- Religious or inspirational images
- Scenics
- Science and technology
- Sports
- Travel
- Weather
- Wildlife

How to Sell Stock Photos

If you're seriously interested in developing stock photograph sales, obtain a copy of the *American Society of Media Photographers Stock Photography Handbook.* This comprehensive guide provides a wealth of information on how to go about selling stock photos. Here are some brief guidelines to follow.

The first step in selling stock photos is to have a large enough body of work from which to choose between two hundred and four hundred images for submission to a stock agency. "The more photos in your submission the better," recommends Tim Potter, director of international operations for the stock agency MT USA. "However, tightly edit your work to your best areas of expertise—

don't show us a little of everything. We look for very strong, thematic work. We've signed contracts with some people for only five photos and up to five hundred."

He says that most stock agents prefer 35 mm transparencies (slides), although some specify four-by-five negatives, and many are now accepting images in high-resolution digital formats. If you're sending slides, have them duplicated, and be sure to send the copies rather than the originals.

Tim also recommends sending photos via express services and including a self-addressed stamped envelope or Federal Express account number with your submission. "It will greatly speed up the return process and show us you're a fair and organized business person," he adds.

"A cover letter with your bio or resume is very helpful; tear sheets and other printed samples are also nice, as are photo books you may have published. Most agencies, like ourselves, publish catalogs to market our photos, so keep in mind that these catalogs aren't done overnight and that your photos may not get to market for six to twelve months, depending on when you submit them."

Stock Photos Online

The Internet is a major source for both royalty-free and traditional stock photography and, therefore, a terrific resource for would-be stock suppliers. Agencies such as PhotoDisc, Corbis, and PictureQuest each represent thousands of photographers. To find these and other stock agencies, use keywords *stock photography agency* at a search engine site such as Google (www.google.com). Most have links to pages that tell you how to submit your portfolios, what the agency is looking for, and what kind of remuneration you might receive.

Inventory Your Photographs

Once you're satisfied with your body of work, develop an inventory that includes the following information for each image: the subject, the date, the medium (black and white or color, slide or digital or transparency), the place it was taken, whether you have a model or property release (a release is required if there are people, pets, or personal property that can be recognized in the photograph), and any other pertinent information. A printed list with this information is essential for developing sales, and it's very helpful to organize your images and lists by subject matter.

Label slides with your name, phone number, a copyright mark (for example, Copyright © 2003 Cheryl McLean), and either the title, subject matter, or an inventory number that corresponds to your list. Many photographers who work extensively in stock have developed computerized database inventories that help keep track of the images in their collections, where they've been sold, and, if so, what rights were sold. If you're using a computer database, include an entry field for keywords. Your database then becomes an efficient and powerful tool for finding just the right image for a specific need. For example, if you have a photo of a little girl playing with a red ball and a golden retriever in the snow, your keywords might include *dog, cute kid, child, girl, winter, snow, play, ball, red, retriever,* and a reference to the child's ethnicity. Then, when a client calls needing a cute kid shot, it's easy to find.

Select Prospective Agencies

Review available information about stock agencies to determine which are appropriate markets for your work. *Photographer's Market* lists some 240 agencies with specific information about their subject needs, submission guidelines, and payment policies.

Write to the agency to request submission guidelines, subject needs, and, if possible, a stock catalog. It's important to try to match your photographs with the appropriate stock agency to increase the likelihood of a sale.

Talk with other photographers (the agency should provide a list if you request one) about what it is like to work with the agency. You want to be sure you are working with an agency that pays regularly and promptly, that actively sells the work in its collection—not just the work of its top photographers—and that concentrates in your areas of specialty. You'll also want to avoid agencies that charge excessive fees, sell rights for use of the photos to clients at large discounts, offer substantially less than the standard 50 percent commission, or do not offer access to audit records for verifying sales in the case of a dispute.

One photographer who specializes in stock photos suggests consulting the Picture Agency Council of America Directory (www.pacaoffice.org). The PACA has established a standard code of ethics, to which member agencies subscribe. In addition, look for the *Photo District News* annual issue on stock photography trends and concerns.

Making the Sale

After you submit your work for review, you'll get an offer from the agency if the editor feels your work merits inclusion in the collection. Arrangements between photographers and stock agencies involve written contracts, which you should consider negotiable documents. Review them carefully. Consider all the elements before you sign.

Most photographers will refuse to sign an exclusive arrangement with a stock agency, though some agency reps will tell you this is standard procedure. An exclusive contract means that you can only sell your work through the agency. This is not a very good deal from your perspective.

Once you've reviewed the terms and signed the contract, you've established a relationship with an agency that will now review your work regularly when you submit it. The agency will also send you regular reports of photo sales along with payment for your commission.

The Move to Digital

Don Landwehrle has thousands of photographic images in his own library, which he converted to Photo CD. He does both assignment and stock photography, which he processes on his extensive computer system.

"The assignment end of my work is what paid for the equipment," he says. "I've always had the belief that if the job would pay for (or close to) the equipment, then buy the equipment and do the job."

For assignment work, Don shoots with a four-by-five camera, then takes the transparencies to a service bureau to scan them on a drum scanner. After manipulating the images with Photoshop, he sends the client a file instead of outputting a chromalin print, or chrome.

"I still find most clients have to be talked out of outputting to chromes and staying digital," Don adds, "but after talking to them and telling them the benefits, they will go with a digital file."

The benefits are primarily in the reproduction quality. By keeping the photograph in its digital form, the designer is working, essentially, with an original image. Every step in the traditional printing process involved getting one step further from the original image. The digital file allows there to be only two steps: from computer to printing plate to the printed page.

The Freelance Assistant

Many professional photographers with large corporate contracts for complex projects require the services of assistants. This offers aspiring professionals a chance to learn the ropes working with an experienced photographer.

Freelance assistants are self-employed and can earn from $50 to $300 per day, based on experience and knowledge and the work required from the photographer. Someone hired to put film in the camera will not earn as much as someone responsible for assisting with staging, lighting, or processing and printing.

A Freelance Assistant's Experiences

Peter Archer is a freelance assistant who works in the Washington, D.C., area. Although he started out in a college art photography program, he left to work in a camera store, where he learned a lot about cameras and photography. He recommends business courses to anyone wanting to freelance for a living, either as a photographer or through the stepping-stone approach of working as an assistant. Design courses, too, are useful because they help you speak the same language as the designers who hire you.

"Assisting has allowed me to travel fairly extensively while working on photographic projects and getting paid a relatively fair wage," Peter says.

As a freelance assistant, Peter does just about everything the photographer would do plus run out for lunch. He looks for angles for shots and watches to make sure the lights are firing, the camera is set correctly, the film is going through the camera, the subject's clothes are straight, and all the client's needs are met. He runs errands and takes the film in for processing. "The only thing we really don't usually do," he says, "is get the clients and push the button on the camera."

Peter's advice for getting jobs as an assistant is to get to know every photographer you come into contact with and be so good at what you do that when a photographer is stuck and needs someone to help, you're the one to be called. This approach also works for developing clients on your own, once you've gained experience. It's unethical to steal clients from the photographers you work for, but if they're unable or choose not to take a job and the client turns to you, you want to be ready to jump at it.

Assisting gives a freelancer the opportunity to explore a variety of photographic areas. You might work with a commercial photographer one day on a fashion magazine spread and with an architectural photographer the next day.

"The advantages of assisting are that you learn everything about being a photographer except the unlearnables," says Peter, "which include the 'eye' and the 'schmooze' factor. The downside is that you reach a certain point where you can do anything the photographer can do and it's all you can do to keep from throttling photographers who are obviously incompetent. Then it's time to move on and start shooting on your own."

Darkroom Work

If you've set up your own darkroom and enjoy working with this part of the process, you can earn extra income by processing and printing the film of other photographers and amateurs.

Davis Photo is a father-and-daughter operation in the elder Davis's garage-turned-darkroom. What began as a personal hobby and then grew to supplement other full-time work has become a thriving business. Bill and his daughter Janet work exclusively with black and white and are the only black-and-white film processors in their community of forty-five thousand.

They process and print film, contact sheets, and prints ranging in size from two by two inches to eleven by fourteen. In addition to standard processing, they handle copy work, make black-and-white prints from color slides or prints, and take product photographs for a variety of commercial clients.

They have also expanded into the computer graphics field with the addition of a film scanner and computer as well as a printer that can prepare color slides and transparencies for presentations. They have been surprised at the rapid growth of their business in this field and have had to take on an additional staff person to handle the demand.

The Business of Freelancing

If you're going to work on your own, you need to explore some of the business aspects of working independently. One of your first investments should be voice mail or a telephone answering system so that you will never miss a call from a prospective client.

An E-mail account is another must. Many businesspeople rely heavily on E-mail communications for convenience and cost efficiency. It's important to check your E-mail daily, because when the client makes the initial contact, you need to respond quickly be ready to get down to business. Here are some important areas for you to understand.

Business Expenses

We've talked about the income possibilities, but what about the expenses? One of the most frequent mistakes freelancers make is to focus on how much they made without taking into account how much it cost them to earn money in the first place. There are a number of business details that can't be ignored if you're going to succeed as a freelancer.

Setting Your Rates

When you set your prices, at first you're going to be looking at the value of the experience, the line on the resume, the photo credit. But eventually you need to move your bottom line a little closer to the one at the bank. Of course you need to keep track of your expenses—travel costs, film, processing, model fees, postage, assistant payment—for specific jobs. But that's not all. You need to consider all of your monthly or annual expenses—rent for studio or darkroom space, utilities such as electric and telephone, insurance, photography and office equipment, taxes, dues for professional memberships, supplies. Then try to estimate, realistically, how many assignments you can complete or sales you can make on a regular basis. Then you can calculate how much you need to bill each week or each month in order to break even. All of these variables will help you determine how to set your rates.

Taxes

As a freelancer, whenever you earn more than $400 with no taxes withheld, it is subject to self-employment tax, which is essentially the same as Social Security tax. Keeping track of your expenses is essential because this helps reduce the level of income that is subject to tax. Deductible expenses include virtually anything that is used exclusively for your business: equipment purchase or rental, employee salaries, supplies, professional services, representative fees, self-promotional brochures, or business cards. Your home office or darkroom is also deductible, provided the space is dedicated solely to business use.

For more information on taxes and the business side of free-lancing, the IRS provides several relevant publications: *Tax Guide for Small Businesses, Business Expenses, Business Use of Your Home,* and *Self-Employment Tax.* To obtain copies of these booklets, call the toll-free IRS number listed in your local directory or visit the Internet site at www.irs.gov.

Copyright Basics

You need to become well versed in the intricacies of rights sales to protect yourself and your future income as a photographer. The moment you develop the film or print an image, it is ostensibly copyrighted. You don't need to register an image with the U.S. Copyright Office in order to obtain legal protection unless you are preparing to file suit against a photo buyer for copyright infringement. Infringement means someone is using your photograph without your permission.

Selling Rights. When you sell a photograph to a client, you are not necessarily selling all rights to that photograph. You want to be able to sell it again to other clients or use it yourself in self-promotional pieces. In essence, you're "renting" your photograph to someone to use for a specifically defined purpose. Ownership of the copyright should remain yours. To retain ownership, however, you need to be diligent in understanding the rights that you offer for sale when you sell individual photographs or your photographic services to a client.

Copyright Law. In 1989, the U.S. Supreme Court affirmed the standards of copyright ownership for all creative works, including photography, established in the Copyright Law of 1976. Ownership can be transferred only by written agreement.

To help ensure copyright protection, be sure to mark everything you send out with the international copyright symbol, ©, followed by the year in which the photograph was taken and your name. In addition, you might want to include the phrase "All rights reserved." A computer labeling program or a rubber stamp and indelible ink pad will help to simplify this process.

Basic Rights Definitions. The rights that photographers might offer for sale include the following:

- **All rights.** This involves selling the right for the buyer to use the photograph in any way and as often as desired for a specified or unspecified period of time.
- **Exclusive rights.** The buyer is the only one, including the photographer, who can use the photograph. Exclusive rights can be negotiated by time period and by specific use, however. For example, a client might negotiate to keep a photograph from being used by a competing company in the same industry for the period of one year.
- **First rights.** The client is buying the right to be the first to use the photograph. The price for first rights is generally a little higher because the buyer is paying to be the first to use it. Obviously first rights can be sold only once.
- **One-time rights.** The client is buying the right to use the photograph only once.
- **Promotion rights or agency promotion rights.** This allows the buyer to use the photograph in materials that promote the publication in which the photograph originally appeared. Agency promotion rights give the stock agency or advertising agency permission to use the photograph in its self-promotion.
- **Serial rights or first serial rights.** These terms relate to the right to use the photograph in a periodical or magazine. First serial rights are generally priced higher than subsequent serial rights sales and can be sold only once.
- **Work for hire.** According to the Copyright Act, this is "a work prepared by an employee within the scope of employment; or a work specially ordered or commissioned for use . . . if the parties expressly agree in a written

instrument signed by them that the work shall be considered a work made for hire." A work made for hire means the photographer permanently relinquishes all rights to the photographs created under the terms of the contract, as well as rights to any future compensation or royalties. Staff photographers, by definition, do work for hire.

Additional Copyright Information. Other resources include the subdivision of American Society of Media Photographers (ASMP) devoted to issues of copyright, Media Photographers Copyright Association (MPCA). The *ASMP Copyright Guide for Photographers* by Richard Weisgrau and Michael Remer is available from the association and can be accessed from its website at www.asmp.org. The National Press Photographers Association also provides answers to frequently asked questions about copyright issues and rights sales on its website, www.nppa.org.

The U.S. Copyright Office also has a variety of publications available explaining copyright laws. The website provides answers to frequently asked questions as well as a form for requesting specific documents. To register a photograph, you need Form VA (visual artist works). The cost for filing a copyright registration is $10, so registering every image is impractical, but if you have images with a high risk of infringement and a high income potential, it may be worth the investment. For forms and information, contact:

Register of Copyrights
Library of Congress
Washington, DC 20059
www.lcweb.loc.gov

Finding Clients

In addition to the prospects described above, don't forget about some of the more obvious resources for finding clients who might need your photographs. At the local library, you'll find a number of trade directories that list names, addresses, and phone numbers of corporations, manufacturers, periodicals, and book publishers. Often these are indexed by geographic region. Some of these references include *Standard Directory of Advertisers, Adweek Directory of Advertising Agencies, Literary Marketplace, Ayer Directory of Publications, Standard Rate & Data Guide,* and *Bacon's Publicity Checker.*

For More Information

Organizations

International Freelance Photographers Organization
P.O. Box 777
Lewisville, NC 27023
www.aipress.com
> (*Membership includes a subscription to* Today's Photographer, *an online magazine for freelancers.*)

Society of Photographer & Artist Representatives (SPAR)
60 East Forty-Second Street, Number 1166
New York, NY 10165
> (*The Society of Photographer and Artist Representatives offers a package of sample forms and copyright explanations that can be very useful when you're negotiating your own rights sales. It's called the SPAR Do-It-Yourself Kit and is available direct from the Society.*)

American Society of Media Photographers
14 Washington Road, Suite 502
Princeton Junction, NJ 08550
www.asmp.org

Volunteer Lawyers for the Arts
One East Fifty-Third Street, Sixth Floor
New York, NY 10022
www.vlan.org

Editorial Photographers
P.O. Box 591811
San Francisco, CA 94159
www.editorialphoto.com

American Institute of Graphic Arts (AIGA)
164 Fifth Avenue
New York, NY 10010
www.aiga.org

Society for Photographic Education (SPE)
101 Art Building
Miami University
Oxford, OH 45056
www.spenational.org

Books

ASMP Professional Business Practices in Photography. Allworth
   Press.
Business and Legal Forms for Photographers, by Tad Crawford.
   Allworth Press.
Legal Guide for the Visual Artist, by Tad Crawford. Allworth Press.
*Legal Handbook for Photographers: The Rights and Liabilities of
   Making Images,* by Bert P. Krages, Esq. Amherst Media.
*Photographer's Market Guide to Photo Submission and Portfolio
   Formats,* by Michael Willins. Writer's Digest Books.
Photographer's Market. Writer's Digest Books.

Pricing Photography: The Complete Guide to Assignment & Stock Prices, by Michal Heron and David MacTavish. Allworth Press.

Sell and Resell Your Photos: How to Sell Your Pictures to a World of Markets a Mailbox Away (4th ed.), by Rohn Engh. Writer's Digest Books.

The Big Picture: The Professional Photographer's Guide to Rates, Rights and Negotiation, by Lou Jacobs Jr. Writer's Digest Books.

The Photographer's Guide to Marketing and Self-Promotion, by Maria Piscopo. Allworth Press.

The Professional Photographer's Management Handbook, by Ann Montieth. Marathon Press.

CHAPTER SEVEN

On the Road Again

Travel Photography

If you have a bit of wanderlust, like to explore new locales and use your camera to document the scenery, architecture, and people of the world, then travel photography could be your passport to a rewarding career. But travel photography isn't always about exotic ports of call. Any location is a potential travel opportunity for people from somewhere else. Even photographs of your hometown can sell as travel shots to a variety of clients.

The ideal situation for a travel photographer is a long-standing relationship with one or more major clients who send you to a broad array of locales and pick up the tab for airfare, hotels, and meals, as well as film and a hefty day rate. What is far more common is that you pay your own way to locations you wanted to visit anyway with the hope that you'll sell some photos on your return—maybe enough to pay for your film, developing, and a few miscellaneous expenses. Fortunately, there is a fair amount of middle ground between these extremes.

Bob Krist, one of the top travel photographers in the country, provides some delightful insight on the real life of a travel photographer. He has published extensively in all the major travel magazines, and he contributed a column to *Travel & Leisure* magazine for several years. He describes an average assignment:

"Average assignment is almost a contradiction in terms, but most editorial assignments start with either an idea that I generate and pitch to an editor or an assignment that crosses an editor's desk and then he or she calls me (hopefully) or whoever they want to use.

"The phone call usually begins with, 'How would you like to go to _____?' Then you say 'yes' (you can't say 'no'). Then you begin the long, tedious task of researching and planning the trip. I spend an average of two days researching for every day I spend in the field. Phone calls, tracking down leads, reading previous articles about the place, finding guides or local help, checking out the minutiae of transport, begging help with expenses from tourist boards, packing equipment into smaller and smaller cases, getting shots and prescriptions. If you have any energy left to take pictures when you finally arrive, you've passed the first hurdle.

"Then you've got jet lag, driving on the wrong side of the road, language barriers, bribes and tips, and being completely lost and disoriented to deal with. Then you have to take some great pictures.

"Then you get home. You've got jet lag, kid bribery, familial responsibilities, plus a couple hundred rolls of film to process, edit, and caption. Then you've got to do your expenses and remember how many rupees you gave that bellhop to let you onto the hotel roof. Then you get your tray of slides together and venture into no-man's-land—the editor's office—where you lay three weeks of blood, sweat, dysentery, and tears out in front of the assembled jurors and await your fate. Thumbs up, you live to get another assignment. Thumbs down, and it's back to driving a cab."

The Primary Market: Travel Magazines

Travel magazines rarely employ staff photographers to fill their pages, so they rely extensively on freelancers to provide the images essential for enticing readers to new travel experiences. Still, the competition is fierce, and the number of publications devoted to travel is fairly limited.

Larger-circulation magazines with reputations for quality are the hardest nuts to crack, but they also offer the most substantial rewards. *National Geographic,* the pinnacle for any magazine photojournalist or travel photographer, does not review work sent in by freelancers, but a less well-known magazine, *The World & I Magazine*, uses freelancers for half of its approximately 250 photos in each issue. Pretty good odds. Several of the smaller state travel magazines, such as *Oregon Coast Magazine*, *Our State: About North Carolina*, and *Mountain Living*, use freelance photos almost exclusively. These smaller magazines and regional publications probably offer the best initial opportunities for publication and portfolio building and are more likely to try new photographers, especially someone with fresh story ideas and a strong personal portfolio.

Where to Find Travel Magazines

Aside from browsing through supermarket newsstands, perhaps the best source of information for potential magazine clients is *Photographer's Market*. Published by Writer's Digest Books, it's updated annually, and its listings include information about what the magazines publish, what they look for in photographs, how to submit, and what they pay. *Standard Rate and Data Guide* and *Bacon's Publicity Checker*, available in libraries, include consumer and trade magazines with addresses and circulation sizes. It's up to you to make contact to determine editorial content, submission guidelines, and freelance hiring and payment policies.

Many of the smaller and more accessible magazines will be regional, state, or city publications, such as the *Roanoker*, *Ohio Magazine*, *San Diego Family Magazine*, *Vermont Magazine*, *Dakota Outdoors*, *The Chesapeake Bay Magazine*, or *Pennsylvania Magazine*. Many such magazines are published through government offices. For example, *Texas Highways* is produced by the Texas Department of Transportation. Some exotic locations have their own travel publications: *Hawaii Magazine*, *Islands*, and *Caribbean Travel and Life*. Most of these publications use freelance photographs, either supplied on speculation, by assignment, or through stock sales, and they often have ancillary products, such as calendars or greeting cards, that could mean additional income for images with special aesthetic appeal.

How to Get Started with Magazines

Once you get the name of a potential magazine client, call or write for submission guidelines and a sample copy or two. Review the publication carefully to determine its editorial "slant" with the photographs it publishes.

I once made a classic mistake when I was just getting started in the business. I had written an article about touring the potteries in Stoke on Trent, England, for a magazine in the United States. It was an assignment (meaning the editor agreed ahead of time to publish it), but I wasn't going to be reimbursed for expenses.

I'd shot several rolls of the intriguing bottle ovens that once dominated the entire landscape of the area (and contributed to the black coal dust that still lingers on many buildings). I had captured what I thought were great "arty" shots: beautiful bottle-shaped brick structures against dramatic skies and Industrial Revolution–era brick buildings; shards of expensive Wedgwood pottery discarded in a turn-of-the-century wooden wheelbarrow; row upon row of teapots and soup tureens. The lighting, depth of field, balance, composition—everything was perfect.

When I met with the editor, he flipped through the prints I'd made, reviewed the contact sheets, then looked up and said, "Where are the people?" He was incredulous.

Without another word, he pulled out a copy of the magazine and directed me to page through it. I immediately caught on to what I had failed to notice before—*all* of the photographs the magazine published had people in them. Even landscape shots had a body in the foreground.

The story eventually ran, but with stock photos rather than mine. All I got paid was the kill fee—in this case 25 percent of the original total for the assignment. It pays to know your market thoroughly. (Believe it or not, I did live to get other assignments from that editor, and you can bet I had people in every shot!)

Reviewing the publication gives you other valuable information as well: the name of the photo editor (essential—and be sure to spell it correctly), the balance of color and black-and-white, the preferred focal length, whether they print credit lines on photos, and, if you go back far enough, a good sense of what's already been done, as well as what there is that you could suggest.

....

Secondary Markets: General Consumer and Trade Publications, Newspapers, and Book Publishers

Photographer's Market, again, can provide information on other publications that are on the lookout for travel photos, although it will require scouring the listings because they have not been indexed by subject matter.

Consumer Magazines

Consumer magazines—those sold on the newsstands to a general readership—are often targeted to specific groups of consumers, based on interests (*PC World, Backpacker, Fly Fishing, Easyriders*) or age, gender, or other demographics (*Seventeen, Senior Magazine, Working Woman, Family Life*). Don't forget the photography magazines, such as *Petersen's Photographic, Popular Photography, Photo Life, Photo Techniques,* and *Photo World.* The pay may not be as high as for major travel magazines ($50 to $150 per photo average), but the production standard is high and will provide tear sheets you could show any prospective client.

Trade Magazines

Quite a few trade magazines—publications directed to specific industry or consumer groups—include articles on travel for their readers, especially those directed to a more affluent readership. Travel industry publications such as *Recommend Worldwide,* directed at travel agents, hoteliers, meeting planners, and agencies, include travel photography almost exclusively.

Newspapers

Newspapers, especially larger papers with Sunday editions, frequently include a travel section. Even small-town weeklies publish occasional travel stories—a new theme park or hiking trail, a renovated downtown, or a winter ski story. Each represents a story with a "news hook" that makes it sellable. Close-to-home stories like these can be a good introduction to travel photography work. If you can put together a strong package of several photographs that present a varied yet representative picture of the location, your chances of selling it to the newspaper are good.

Newspaper magazine supplements are also a strong travel market and a likely place for color. These sections also more often run travel features on foreign destinations. While newspapers, unlike magazines, employ staff photographers, they'll use freelancers, especially for locations away from the publication's city.

Because of the regionality of newspapers, you can often sell the same story and/or photos to several dailies at once. This doesn't work for the major-market newspapers that have national distribution, such as *USA Today* or even the *New York Times*, which is sold the same day on newsstands around the country.

Books

Book publishers often contract with authors to provide text for forthcoming books, then they rely on the graphic department to arrange photographs or illustrations. Textbooks especially geography and foreign language texts, require a number of images that might come from a travel photographer's stock collection.

The dream of publishing a coffee table book of travel or destination photos is realized by only a handful of photographers, but it's not impossible. If you've got a unique idea coupled with stunning photographs—and there's nothing on the market that meets this need—your chances of finding a publisher are improved.

Preparing Your Presentation Package

The Portfolio

Once you have a solid understanding of the publication and its style, put together a selection of your photographs that will show the editor that you can provide the kind of pictures they publish. Putting together a different portfolio for each potential client might seem onerous, but if the client has the potential of being a major player in your future income, it's worth the extra effort. Remember, too, that the best portfolios demonstrate your originality and commitment to both strong images and technical excellence. (See Chapters 3 and 12 for more specifics on the portfolio.)

Organize your photographs into a sequence that is interesting and revealing of the range of your work. Look at the relationship of photographs in your portfolio—images that face each other on two-page spreads should strike an aesthetic balance, not a jarring discord. Be sure there's a balance of horizontal and vertical shots. Because of the format of virtually all magazines on the market, if you want to get a cover shot or a full-page image on the inside, it's going to have to be vertical.

Ideas and Cover Letters

The next step is to develop a list of several good ideas for stories that would make a perfect fit with the publication you're interested in shooting for. Some publications won't review portfolios unless they're submitted for consideration with a particular story idea. Your cover letter needs to present your ideas, your experience, and your special skills—all in a single page. If possible, present all this information in person.

Presenting Your Portfolio

If you live in New York (which is still the heart of the publishing industry) or another city with a high concentration of travel publications, take the time to make personal phone calls to set up appointments with photo editors to show your work. If you're traveling to one of these cities, plan well in advance and try to set up meetings with as many prospective clients as possible. Your goal is to establish long-term relationships with clients who think of you when an assignment comes around.

Sometimes, especially with new photographers, a magazine's policy requires you to drop off your portfolio and then wait for a phone call. Include your business card and a self-promotional postcard or flyer, which the editor can keep after reviewing your work. You want to leave a visual reminder, as well as all the standard information about how to reach you for assignments. If you haven't invested in a personal promotional piece, you could leave some tear sheets from previously published work or a few color photocopies of photographs for the editor to keep on file.

Travel pro Bob Krist describes additional strategies. "I also get jobs by informing a broad range of clients and near clients of my upcoming travel plans. If they have a story coming up in an area in which I'll be working, they often will 'piggyback' their assignment onto my existing job, thereby saving the travel expenses."

Even if you don't live in the Big Apple, in the age of overnight package delivery, fax, and E-mail, there's no reason for you to feel limited in your markets—whether you live in Tuscaloosa, Oklahoma, or Washougal, Washington. Write a query letter, again following submission guidelines, presenting a couple of dynamite ideas along with your portfolio. Check submission guidelines to determine whether previously published photographs are acceptable. If so, you might want to indicate the availability of stock travel photographs. An index by location and subject matter will be an important tool for selling stock photos to the travel market.

The Tourism Industry

The tourism industry—tour guides, cruise ships, airlines, major hotel chains, resorts, and travel agencies—is an important potential market for the travel photographer. More commercial than editorial or personal, tourism photography is involved with presenting a specific "product," whether the destination served by an airline, the fabulous food spreads on an ocean liner, or the elegant lobby of a first-class hotel.

Resorts and attractions, such as Disneyland and Six Flags, have been producing glossy self-promotion pieces and advertisements for years, but travel destinations themselves—cities and states—

are getting in on the self-promotion act. In my home state of Oregon, tourism has become the third largest industry and is rapidly gaining on the number-two position currently held by forest products. The state's Office of Tourism prepares a broad array of photo-drenched publications to keep the visitors coming.

This is a story being repeated across Canada and the United States in regions of particular natural beauty or historic interest. Our countries are on the move, and cities, states, and provinces all over are clamoring for the wandering populace to come by for a visit. Chambers of commerce, tourism bureaus, and economic development offices are all preparing slick publications and advertisements that put the best scenic foot forward. To do this, they need your beautiful photographs.

The Tourism Product

In each of these situations, the "product" is paramount, but inevitably the client will want photographs showing people actively and quite thoroughly enjoying the product—so much so that it makes the viewer want to rush right out and buy tickets to go there. As you shoot, remember to keep in the front of your mind what it is that would make this situation appealing. Avoid showing crowds, unless it's an audience enjoying a performance.

Don't bother taking photographs in the rain, because most likely they won't be used—even if you're covering a rain forest. Chances are the image that will run shows the sun glistening off dewdrops the moment the rain stops. Shoot interiors if it's raining, but let the sun come out before you venture outside.

And never let the disturbing side of any travel experience creep into your corporate tourism photographs. While it might work in a photo essay for a newspaper to show hungry, begging children surrounding a tourist, it is most definitely not part of the "sell" for encouraging visitors to travel to that particular destination. Travel photography, unlike photojournalism, is involved with capturing an ideal and involving viewers to the extent that they feel part of the image, or at least that they would like to be.

Stock Travel Photography

Although Chapter 6 deals with stock photography in greater depth, this is a market the travel photographer should not overlook. Many professional travel photographers also shoot stock to expand the revenue potential from any travel experience. A very few work exclusively as stock photographers, traveling to exotic locations to develop stock images according to specialized market needs or the demands of current trends.

Stock travel photos give clients a "safe" buy. They don't have to invest in a day rate or costly travel expenses for a photographer who may or may not be able to deliver what they're looking for. (You can't always count on bright sunshine on the northern coast of Scotland or even snow drifts in Vermont.) If they can find an image that already exists, so much the better. Sometimes stock photos provide the only solution for a company that needs a New Orleans Mardi Gras photo in July or needs an image now and can't wait for the time it takes to send a photographer on location.

What It Takes

A good travel photographer needs to enjoy more than just taking pictures in diverse settings. Depending on your client, you need strong social skills as well. Knowing how to get around in a variety of cultures and settings is a valuable trait in this field. Juggling equipment, passports, tickets, and train schedules takes a certain degree of physical and temperamental stamina. You should also keep abreast of U.S. State Department travel advisories about safety conditions for citizens abroad. Sometimes the political climate can make international travel conditions hazardous. Canadian citizens should contact the Department of External Affairs.

People Skills

Getting perfect strangers to let you photograph them and having them walk away happy with you—and, by extension, the magazine—can play an important role in the final quality of your images. This is even more important for tourism photography, where you are photographing people in the process of enjoying (and having paid for) your client's services. You can't get in the way of their holiday, but if you approach it right, you can become part of their fun and memories while getting natural "models" for your photographs without paying model's fees. (If your client is picking up expenses, it's a good idea to offer lunch or a drink to people who go out of their way to help you get your photographs.)

Model Release Forms

Another part of working with people, particularly when working for tourism clients, is getting them to sign a model release form giving permission for their likenesses to be published in the magazine, in promotional publications, or, in some cases, for unlimited promotional use. This is required whether you've used a professional model or taken advantage of people present on the scene (as long as the person is recognizable). A lesser-known fact is that if you can recognize a pet or private property in a photograph intended for advertising, these, too, require release forms from their owners. Negotiating a release is essential; without one, you may have wasted your time taking the photographs. A corporate client can't use people's likenesses for advertising without written permission (the legal term is *appropriation*), and many magazine publishers won't.

Technically, for editorial publications, if someone is in a public place, there is no legal basis for objecting to one's image being published as part of an article in a publication. If the person is in a public place, there is no "right to privacy" that is being violated; similarly, if the article is for editorial purposes rather than commercial (advertising), there is no "appropriation." However, many publishers prefer that photographers receive written permission to prevent misunderstandings and avoid harassment suits.

The Photographer's Personal Image

If you're being sent out on assignment by a magazine, chances are the editor will take into account the image you present. Can you fit into the environment you'll be working in? Are you presentable? Will you be able to arrange permission to photograph when you're on the spot and you've run into someone who doesn't want to let you through to your destination?

Technical Expertise

As with any area of photography in which you are trying to sell your skills or finished photographs, technical expertise is a given. When you're shooting the moonrise over Ama Dablam in Nepal or catching a surfer in the curl of a big wave on Oahu's Banzai Pipeline, you don't have time to wonder about f-stops or the best lens for the job. You need to understand your equipment so well that these decisions are second nature.

Take Plenty of Pictures

Another consideration when on assignment is to be sure you present a lot of options. When working as an intern for the travel section of a major magazine, I went on my first assignment with one of the magazine's standard freelance photographers. We knew when we started that the story would run one column with one black-and-white photo. The photographer, Michael Thompson, shot six rolls of thirty-six exposures, with a dozen or more shots of each situation. When I asked why he took so many, he explained that it's a lot cheaper for the company to buy and process several rolls of film than to pay his day rate and travel expenses to reshoot. The magazine's editors aren't going to settle for something that merely "works"—even for a relatively insignificant shot for a small story.

Photographer/Writer Advantage

Some magazines prefer to have story/photo packages submitted, but both pieces of the package must be top-notch. Toward this end, you might want to develop a relationship with a writer, if your skills don't extend to the written word.

John and Ellin Saverin work together as a team—he's a writer, she's a photographer—and they both have a deep love of travel and adventure that has taken them to every continent on the globe. Their clients have included a major corporation that wanted to document the building of a new factory in Asia with words and pictures; a cruise line that needed a dynamic travel brochure to send to its corporate clients; and a whole host of magazines, some of which are dedicated to travel but many that just liked the ideas John and Ellin had to offer.

"The key is coming up with a new angle, a new way of looking at something, or an 'undiscovered' destination," says Ellin. She and her writer husband have brainstorming meetings over morning coffee at least twice a week to come up with ideas.

"Sometimes we work on coming up with ideas to go with places we want to travel to; then we look for the client who might be interested," Ellin adds. "Other times, we focus on the client first and develop ideas to fit that particular market."

Either way, it's a strategy that has paid off. John and Ellin manage to work ten months of the year, then spend their two free months traveling for themselves. "Although I have to admit we're never really on vacation," she says. "Wherever we go, I'm shooting pictures and John's taking notes in his ever-present notebook. But very often these turn into jobs we can sell when we get back, so it's worth it."

Income Potential

The rate of pay in travel photography depends entirely on the client and can vary wildly. The local newspaper might pay as little as $8 per photograph published; a tourism client might pay close to $1,500 for a stock shot if it's unique; a magazine cover shot might command $2,000. Day rates, too, vary according to the client and your experience. One beginning photographer I worked with charged $20 per hour, or $160 for an eight-hour day; a more experienced regional photographer's day rate was $800; a photographer whose work is in demand might charge $1,200 per day.

Other Benefits

"Comps," or complimentary fares, lodging, or passes, can sometimes be a side benefit for the travel photographer. If you're working on a legitimate travel assignment under contract and the magazine you're working for doesn't pay expenses, you might be able to arrange for discounted or comp travel. Something that would be completely unethical for a photojournalist because of the need to be unbiased becomes more acceptable for the travel photographer because of the underlying assumption that the finished piece won't include "negative" photographs. If you're on assignment, check with the editor, however, to be sure there are no rules against freelancers accepting comps.

Also, be very clear with the client that you have no control over the final choice of photographs to be published. You might offer to send prints (marked clearly with your copyright and the statement "For Personal Use Only") as a partial compensation.

Working Under Contract

When working on assignment, get the terms in writing. Ask which rights the client is buying (see Chapter 6 for a discussion of rights sales). Find out whether expenses will be reimbursed and what is included in billable expenses—air, other transportation, personal car miles, lodging, meals, film, and processing.

If your client is paying for expenses, get 50 percent up front and, if possible, arrange to have the balance of expenses paid immediately upon return. Will you be compensated for time spent traveling, editing, and waiting around for the weather to clear? This time is usually billed at a proportion of your day rate.

How many photographs are you contracting for? Is there specific subject matter the client wants? Are there any conditions or limitations that should be spelled out before you begin? Be sure to get all the issues clarified before you take off. The more specific the contract, the less likely there will be misunderstanding and disappointment on either your part or your client's. Sample contract forms are available in a number of publications, as well as from the American Society of Media Photographers (ASMP).

. . . .

Photographing Travelers

Another way to combine a love of travel with a passion for photography is to become the official photographer on a trip. You might be employed with the travel agency that organizes bus tours or by a destination resort or company.

David Callahan is the staff photographer on a six-thousand-passenger cruise ship that tours the Hawaiian Islands half the year and the South Pacific the other half. A graduate of Southwest Oregon Community College with an associate's degree in photographic technology, David wanted to do more than work in a darkroom. "I was a surf bum for a while in Hawaii, and I would take photos of surfing competitions and sell them to magazines or, more often, to individual surfers," he recalls. "But I paid the bills by working in a color photography lab that did everything from one-hour processing to slide duplication, retouching, reprints, and enlargements. Then I got a line on a great job. A friend of mine was the purser for a major cruise company, and there was an opening for a photo technician, someone to make duplicate prints in the onboard photo lab.

"After two years, I was promoted to ship photographer, which is much more fun. I get to interact with the passengers and spend more time on shore excursions. I take shots of individuals and families as they board the ship, action shots of people out having fun, or portraits with the captain on special evenings—women in evening gowns, men in suits and tuxedos. Then I turn the film over to the lab tech, who prints four-by-sixes to display in a special room adjacent to the gift shop. People wander through and find photos of themselves, then order reprints to take home with them. It's a great business!"

Mia Tsutakawa also works on the ocean, but on a much smaller boat. She's the underwater photographer for a company that takes tourists to great snorkeling spots on Maui. A lifelong resident of the islands, Mia is certified as a scuba diver and has a bachelor's degree in oceanography from the University of Hawaii. "In the end," she says, "I was much more passionate about photography than about research, but I couldn't get out of the water! So this job was ideal.

"We take two tours out every day with about eight people on board. The tours go out every day of the week, and we only take about five holidays a year, but the staff rotates, so I usually only work four days a week. Each trip involves at least two dive sessions at two locations. We have a few passengers each trip who do scuba, but most people are snorkelers.

"The divers are the ones paying the most money, so that's who I focus on first. They're also the most likely to want to take home documentation of their trip. I put on my diving gear and move around, catching photos of as many people as possible.

"On some trips, we have an underwater videographer who takes a lot of footage of the first dive and some of the second dive and then, using another computer and iMovie software, puts together a nice video complete with soundtrack that plays on a viewing screen belowdecks as we motor back to port. He takes orders and then makes copies of the video and ships them out the next day.

"I have some pretty sophisticated underwater camera equipment. It's all digital, and we have a computer and photo printer on board, so after each dive session, I upload images from the cameras and make a set of prints of anything that might sell—especially prints that clearly show the individual swimmers or divers surrounded by colorful tropical fish. When we get back in port, while all the work of tying up and stowing gear is happening, I'm frantically putting up a display of the photos so people can view them and decide what they want to buy. I always have some old standby photos—such as a classic sea turtle shot—for people who didn't have their own underwater cameras. The last hour or two is pretty crazy, but we make enough in sales to justify my salary!"

Her educational background gives her an advantage with photographing fish underwater. She can identify fish for the tourists, but she has also built an impressive library of underwater shots that she sells as stock photos to a wide range of clients.

Education and Training

The major hurdle to a photography job within the tourism industry is finding the job opening. The competition for such plum positions is stiff, but the jobs are out there if you're persistent and willing to do a little research. The job requirements for a cruise industry photography position are usually two to three years of professional photography experience, an outgoing personality, sales skills, and a sense of adventure. You must be willing to live on a ship for six to nine months, with four- to eight-week vacations between seasons. Special skills—such as Mia's scuba certification and scientific and computer knowledge—are helpful, too.

Potential Earnings

For a cruise photographer, pay begins at around $1,000 a month for a lab technician, $1,400 for an entry-level photographer, and $2,000 for a photo manager. Often salary is based on commission on sales. In addition, you get free room and board while you're at sea, although the crew accommodations are like windowless college dorm rooms, which you'll share with another crew member. The food is generally pretty good, but you'll dine in the officer's mess rather than the guest dining rooms or restaurants. If you need to travel by air to your port of debarkation, you'll usually have to cover that cost yourself.

For More Information

Organizations

Society of American Travel Writers
1500 Sunday Drive, Suite 102
Raleigh, NC 27607
www.satw.org

Periodicals

Bacon's Publicity Checker
Bacon's Media Directories
332 South Michigan Avenue
Chicago, IL 60604

Outdoor Photographer
12121 Wilshire Boulevard, Suite 1220
Los Angeles, CA 90025
www.outdoorphotographer.com

Books

The Location Photographer's Handbook: The Complete Guide for the Out-of-Studio Shoot, by Ken Haas. John Wiley & Sons.
Panoramic Photography, by Joseph Meehan. Watson-Guptill Publications.
Travel Photography, by Susan McCarthy. Allworth Press.
Travel Photography: A Guide to Taking Better Pictures, by Richard Anson. Lonely Planet Publications.
The Travel Photographer's Handbook: Professional Techniques— The National Geographic Way, by Albert Moldvay et al. Eriako Associates.

CHAPTER EIGHT

Natural Wonders

Nature and Wildlife Photography

I
f your love of nature and wildlife takes you outdoors with your camera, nature photography may be your niche. Getting started in this field takes patience and perseverance, but the benefit of spending your time in the great outdoors has to mean more than a hefty paycheck. In addition to the romantic images of trekking backwoods trails or canoeing crystalline waters in search of elusive wildfowl, the successful nature photographer spends what may seem to be an inordinate amount of time in the office marketing photographs, captioning slides, researching prospective clients, and conducting the business end of the operation.

The Elements of Nature Photography

The wide world is the backdrop for the nature photographer's art, and all the flora and fauna provide the subject matter. Closely associated with painting in its aesthetics, nature photography encompasses sweeping landscapes and scenics as well as super close-ups, taken with a macro lens, of flowers and insects. It also includes the more specific categories of wildlife photography and underwater photography.

Wildlife Photography

Wildlife subjects can range from the chickadee nesting in your backyard to elephants roaming the high plains of Africa, from spiny iguanas on the Galapagos Islands to an aerial view of an eagle's aerie in the Rocky Mountains. The wildlife photographer captures animals, birds, and insects in their natural habitats, providing insight into their lives and behavior patterns.

Underwater Photography

Photographing in the briny deep combines elements of both nature and wildlife photography. Underwater landscapes and plant life offer rich subject matter, as do the fishes and seagoing mammals of both fresh- and saltwater environments.

We usually think of underwater photographers in exotic tropical locations photographing brilliantly colored fish and tiny sea horses. But any underwater environment is an opportunity for a photographer with the necessary skills and equipment.

Perils, Pitfalls, and Plusses

Norbert Wu, a nature photographer with a strong sense of realistic expectations in the field, often writes for *Shutterbug Magazine*. One story in particular outlined "The Hard Truths of Nature Photography." He cautioned would-be nature photographers to take a good look at the trials and tribulations before choosing this career path.

Nature photography, according to Wu, is not all excitement and adventure. You have to spend a lot of time marketing photographs and lining up assignments, not to mention the time spent in the darkroom for photographers who prefer to process their own film.

Nature photography also is not a guaranteed road to riches, nor does it necessarily bring a lot of opportunities for free travel. Norbert explains that his travel is done mostly at his own expense or as the result of speaking engagements rather than photo assignments. He has supplemented his photography income by writing, as well as going on the speakers' circuit. When he does travel, he piggybacks—arranges to photograph in as many destinations en route or in the area as possible, then expends a lot of energy making each of those opportunities pay.

In the end, though, he concludes, "It's still worth it. . . . With hard work and a good eye, it is possible to make a good living at this profession."

....

Environmental Ethics

Photographers out in the field in search of wildlife and the marvels of nature often encounter situations that require an understanding of the ethical implications. The North American Nature Photography Association has developed a document describing the principles of ethical field practices, which is reprinted here with permission.

PRINCIPLES OF ETHICS AND FIELD PRACTICES

NANPA believes that following these practices promotes the well-being of the location, subject, and photographer. Every place, plant, and animal, whether above or below water, is unique, and cumulative impacts occur over time. Therefore, one must always exercise good individual judgment. It is NANPA's belief that these principles will encourage all who participate in the enjoyment of nature to do so in a way that best promotes good stewardship.

ENVIRONMENTAL: KNOWLEDGE OF SUBJECT AND PLACE

- Learn patterns of animal behavior. *Know when not to interfere with animals' life cycles.*
- Respect the routine needs of animals. *Remember that others will attempt to photograph them, too.*
- Use appropriate lenses to photograph wild animals. *If an animal shows stress, move back and use a longer lens.*
- Acquaint yourself with the fragility of the ecosystem. *Stay on trails that are intended to lessen impact.*

SOCIAL KNOWLEDGE OF RULES AND LAWS

- When appropriate, inform managers or other authorities of your presence and purpose. *Help minimize cumulative impacts and maintain safety.*
- Learn the rules and laws of the location. *If minimum distances exist for approaching wildlife, follow them.*

- In the absence of management authority, use good judgment. *Treat the wildlife, plants, and places as if you were their guest.*
- Prepare yourself and your equipment for unexpected events. *Avoid exposing yourself and others to preventable mishaps.*

INDIVIDUAL: EXPERTISE AND RESPONSIBILITIES

- Treat others courteously. *Ask before joining others already shooting in an area.*
- Tactfully inform others if you observe them engaging in inappropriate or harmful behavior. *Many people unknowingly endanger themselves and animals.*
- Report inappropriate behavior to proper authorities. *Don't argue with those who don't care; report them.*
- Be a good role model, both as a photographer and a citizen. *Educate others by your actions; enhance their understanding.*

Getting Started

Margot Conte is a widely published nature photographer who has taught workshops in nature and wildlife photography and hosted the Nature Photography section of America Online's Kodak Photography Forum. She suggests beginners keep their day jobs while they develop a portfolio and potential client base. "I would not expect to pay the bills while breaking into wildlife photography," she advised one photographer interested in getting out of the darkroom and into the field. "Once you've gathered experience, a reputation, and contacts, then hopefully the money will start to come in."

There is a tremendous amount of competition in the field of nature photography, making it hard to rely on as your only source of support. Photographers who want to work solely by their shutters will most likely need to combine their love of nature photography with other areas, such as travel or commercial photography, at least in the beginning.

"In nature photography, you have to make your market; all areas are 'hot' if you can find a different slant and your work is outstanding," Margot adds. "I know one guy who does nothing but specialize in tree frogs, and his work has been published over and over. Now, if you're really a go-getter, specialize in a 'wanted area,' know how to go about marketing your work, and be the best in your specialization. You then have a chance, but you have to be very good, and it is not easy work!"

When you're first trying to get your work exhibited or published, networking with established photographers or others involved in advertising, public relations, or publishing can help get you an introduction.

"There is no question in my mind that it always helps to know someone in your chosen field, especially when it's highly competitive. But," Margot cautions, "once the door has been opened, then it's not 'who you know,' and you better be able to produce and sustain what you're doing. I doubt there are many people who would lend backing to someone who did not have the talent, because it would then look bad for all. So, the final thought is, if you ask for help, be sure that you can deliver the goods."

Learning the Basics

As with any area of photography, the decision to go to school or to learn on your own is an individual one, and only you can determine what you need. Courses in the technical aspects of photography and darkroom work get you off the ground. Workshops on nature photography, too, can be extremely useful, especially if they involve getting out in the field for a lot of hands-on practice. There is no substitute for experience. Developing your own style comes with patience and a lot of practice. Consider the cost of film and developing to be a kind of tuition payment.

"In my opinion, you must know the technical part of photography like the back of your hand," Margot explains. "It is essential in wildlife photography because many times you will not get a second chance: as the eagle is coming in to scoop up a salmon, you should be ready—not figuring out what f-stop or lens you are going to use."

When she had her first show at Abercrombie, the president of Konica came to the show. "I apologized for being such a green-horn and said that I would go to school and bone up," Margot recalls. "He immediately said that I shouldn't. He thought that I had 'natural ability,' and he didn't want someone to come in and try to change that. I never went. What I did was to study photo after photo. I collected and read nature and wildlife photography books that had comments by the photographers."

Recording Your Procedures

Keeping a log when you photograph is an important tool, both for learning from what you're doing in the field—in terms of f-stops and lenses and shutter speeds, as well as the effect of lighting or atmosphere—and for keeping track of what you're shooting for captioning later on. A field notebook works well, but you might also want to carry a small tape recorder. It can save time and be used while you're moving from one spot to another.

"Try shooting at different times of day, with different lenses and angles," Margot advises. "Become as inventive as you can. Using a 200 mm or even 300 mm lens on the subject will give you a totally different aspect, showing not only detail but imaginative images. Don't always choose a perfect day—fog and rain can also bring you wonderful results."

Getting to Know Your Subjects

Part of learning the craft in nature photography is knowing your subject matter. Photographing scenics and landscapes requires some special understanding, especially of the changes of light throughout the day and in different kinds of weather. Experiment and learn what kinds of results you get under different conditions.

If you're interested in photographing wildlife, get to know your subject thoroughly. Know what signs a trumpeter swan gives before it's about to take flight. Know where the likely feeding areas are for the elk you hope to photograph. What time of day will the beaver emerge from its underwater home? Some of the skills taught in wildlife photography workshops might include animal tracking, setting up blinds, wilderness survival, and off-road etiquette.

"If I were to give one word for photographing wildlife, it would be *patience*," Margot explains. "Animals don't keep the same clocks we do, so be prepared for very early mornings, not much midday, and activity again until sunset. Oh, yes, and rain, sun, cold, heat—you name it—conditions you have never dreamed of! For me, it was a whole new, exciting world. The nice thing about it is that you can adapt it to your own lifestyle. Wildlife photography can be done in your backyard or on the great plains and refuges of the world. It's up to you. Unlike being in the same studio all day, you have an unlimited choice of locale."

Equipment

The most common format for nature photography is 35 mm, primarily because of its portability. The lenses you need depend upon the type of photography you're going to be involved with. Scenics and landscapes generally involve wide angle or natural lenses, while wildlife photographs require longer lenses, up to 400 mm. If you want to shoot close-ups of insects or flowers, you'll need a macro lens.

Margot advises that "once you decide, then you should get the sharpest, fastest lens you can afford." You can defeat your purpose in trying to be competitive if you don't have fine lenses.

A monopod is useful if you're using a long lens and have difficulty holding the extra weight. Tripods can be cumbersome in the field, but some photographers work with tripods and trip releases to enable them to capture photographs of birds or other wildlife returning to the nest or den. A blind can be useful, too, for photographing wildlife, although some photographers prefer to take the time to allow the animals to get accustomed to their presence rather than bother with an extra piece of equipment.

The majority of wildlife and nature work that is published today is in color, although most newspapers use primarily black and white. The film should be the slowest possible speed for the available light to increase the sharpness and color range. Slide film rather than print film is the predominant medium.

Digital cameras with the ability to take fifteen to twenty frames in a minute cost a lot more than the typical digital, but when you're trying to capture the perfect image of a bird in flight or a cougar on the run, you'll want that speed. Most photographers who specialize in landscapes and scenics prefer medium-format cameras because of the quality of the final image and the ability to enlarge photographs dramatically without loss of clarity.

Employment Opportunities

Government Agencies

There are some opportunities for wildlife and nature photographers to work as staff photographers, especially if your educational background involves studying your subject matter. For example, Kevin Whitmore, a forestry graduate from Humboldt State College in the California Redwoods, combined his specialized knowledge of forest science with his love of photography in a career with the U.S. Forest Service.

Other government agencies that employ nature and wildlife photographers are the U.S. Fish and Wildlife Service, the National Park Service, the U.S. Department of Agriculture, and the U.S. Department of the Interior, as well as state government agencies with the same functions.

Underwater photographers might find employment with various research stations throughout the world or with the National Oceanic and Atmospheric Administration (NOAA). Employment with government agencies is discussed in Chapter 9.

Private Organizations

Many private and nonprofit organizations have extensive interests in both wildlife and the natural environment. Organizations such as the Smithsonian Institution, the National Geographic Society, the Sierra Club, and large city zoos all employ staff photographers. Underwater photographers might work on special expeditions for Greenpeace or the Cousteau Society. The pay scale for most of these positions, however, is not likely to be high. These nonprofit organizations use their resources primarily to fund the purpose for which they exist, and many times the people on staff come to these positions because they are dedicated to the cause. Employment might also be based on grants for specific projects, terminating when the project is completed. A facility for grant writing could come in handy for keeping yourself employed!

Freelancing

Most wildlife and nature photographers work as independent freelancers, taking assignments from a wide range of clients or selling their photographs through stock agencies. Chapter 6 provides more information on freelance markets, from magazines and newspapers to the publishers of books, greeting cards, and calendars.

For More Information

Organizations

North American Nature Photographers Association (NANPA)
10200 West Forty-Fourth Avenue, Suite 304
Wheat Ridge, CO 80033
www.nanpa.org

Underwater Photographic Society
P.O. Box 2401
Culver City, CA 90231

Books

Galen Rowell's Vision: Art of Adventure Photography, by Galen
   Rowell. Sierra Club Books.
Green Book. A. G. Editions.
   (Annual directory for nature and stock photographers.)
Mountain Light: In Search of the Dynamic Landscape, by Galen
   Rowell. Sierra Club Books.
*Nature and Wildlife Photography: A Practical Guide to How to
   Shoot and Sell,* by Susan McCartney. Allworth Press.
*The Professional Photographer's Guide to Shooting & Selling
   Nature & Wildlife Photos,* by Jim Zuckerman. F&W
   Publications.
Underwater Photography, by Charles Seaborn. Watson-Guptill
   Publications.

Periodicals

Outdoor Photographer
12121 Wilshire Boulevard, Twelfth Floor
Los Angeles, CA 90025
www.outdoorphotographer.com
   *(Published ten times a year for nature, travel, scenic, landscape, and
   wildlife photographers.)*

Guilfoyle Report
A. G. Editions.
41 Union Square West, Suite 523
New York, NY 10003
www.agpix.com
   (Published ten times a year for nature and stock photographers.)

CHAPTER NINE

Serving the Public

Government and Military Photography

If your dream job includes relative security, great benefits, and adequate salary, you may want to consider working for the government. Although security is not absolute in the public sphere, since it's dependent on taxpayers and budgets, the government is a big employer. Federal, local, and state governments provide employees with annual leave, sick leave, and health care benefits.

Salary levels are in some cases lower for civil service jobs than in the private sector, but generally the benefit packages are so good that they make up for the lower pay. If you are hired as a temporary or project employee, however, which is more common with photography than with many other areas, your position may not include the perquisites that are a big part of what makes working for the government so attractive.

Because government often mirrors the private sector, the range of opportunity for photographers is great. Government agencies make use of all types of photography: portrait, industrial, scientific, and public relations or press photography. You might find yourself taking formal portraits of government officials or performing aerial photography for natural resources and civil departments. You may work as a law enforcement or forensics photographer or as a skilled technical photographer involved in satellites and missiles. Virtually all government agencies need the services of a photographer, but relatively few have photographers on staff.

Both in-house and freelance employment are possible with the government, but competition is fierce. The biggest challenge in freelancing may be finding your way through the bureaucracy to the people who need your services. There is wide variance among state and local government procedures for classifying, paying, and hiring photographers, but federal jobs are standardized.

....

Finding Photography Jobs in the Federal Government

There are approximately three thousand photographers working for the federal government. Once you understand how the federal government organizes jobs, the searching and application processes are not that mysterious. All federal jobs are categorized by occupational number "series," and salary is based on "grade."

Grade is determined by education and experience. The job code "GS-1060-5" tells you that the General Schedule (GS) job classification is for the photography series (1060) and the pay scale is 5, which in 2002 means starting at $22,737 per year. Raises within each grade are classified as "steps," which are earned primarily by time spent on the job. The following list shows starting and maximum salaries for the fifteen GS grades.

- GS-1 $14,757–$18,456
- GS-2 $16,592–$20,876
- GS-3 $18,103–$23,350
- GS-4 $20,322–$26,415
- GS-5 $22,737–$29,559
- GS-6 $25,344–$32,949
- GS-7 $28,164–$36,615
- GS-8 $31,191–$40,551
- GS-9 $34,451–$44,783
- GS-10 $37,939–$49,324
- GS-11 $41,684–$54,185
- GS-12 $49,959–$64,944

- GS-13 $59,409–$77,229
- GS-14 $70,205–$91,265
- GS-15 $82,580–$107,357

A Key to the Photography Federal Job Series

When scanning federal job registers, knowing the series number can be essential. Following is a descriptive list of the photography-related job classifications in the federal government.

- **Photography series** (GS-1060) includes jobs involving supervising or performing work dealing with still, video, or film cameras and in processing film and negatives.
- **Photographic Technology series** (GS-1386) includes jobs involving science and engineering fields that utilize photographic technology. The work involves planning, research, design, and development of photographic equipment and techniques.
- **Audiovisual Production series** (GS-1070) includes jobs involved with producing videos and television programs, radio broadcasts, films, slide shows, and multimedia shows.
- **Visual Information series** (GS-1084) involves planning and designing visual materials.
- **Illustrating series** (GS-1020) involves using electronic graphics or computer animation to produce illustrations and can involve retouching photographs.
- **Cartographic Technology series** (GS-1371) involves aerial photography and photogrammetry.

The Range of Opportunity

Most agencies within the federal government use photography in one way or another. From the official White House photographer to the biologist who photographs humpback whales from the air, photography's usefulness as a tool in documentation and presentation is unending.

The potential for opportunities, therefore, can be promising. However, the federal government is a big place with no centralized way to discover how and where your photographic skills can be best applied. You're in for a big research project, whether you are searching for a position within the government or freelance work from the government. Here are a few examples of specialized photography careers within the federal government.

Photogrammetry and Aerial Photography. A source of many jobs within the federal government and military, photogrammetry is described more thoroughly in Chapter 11 on scientific photography. The Defense Mapping Agency (DMA) provides mapping, charting, and geodetic products, services, training, and advising to all elements of the Department of Defense. It also provides nautical charts and marine navigational data to merchant marine and private vessel operators and maintains liaisons with civil agencies and other international mapping, charting, and geodetic activities.

Jobs with the DMA, like many scientific photography jobs, require more than expertise in photographic techniques. Expertise in the fields of cartography, photogrammetry, geodesy, photo-interpretation, remote sensing, and a number of other scientific fields are emphasized in filling positions within the DMA. This is not a field for a general photographer, but for someone who is interested in photography within the sciences, this is a natural fit.

The Bureau of Land Management, the U.S. Forest Service, and the U.S. Geological Survey also employ photogrammetrists and aerial photographers. If you can pilot a plane as well as photograph, all the better, according to Ron Jameson, a marine biologist with the U.S. Environmental Protection Agency. Aerial photographers are needed frequently for biological and natural resource work.

The most common positions for photogrammetrists and aerial photographers begin at the GS-5 to GS-10 level, or $22,737 to $37,939 annually.

Medical Photography. Medical photographers have many opportunities for positions in the federal government. Every Veterans Administration hospital requires photographers. Norma Jessup is a medical photographer (GS-1060-7) at the Northampton, Massachusetts, Veterans Administration Hospital.

"I perform photography of patients, pathological specimens, autopsies, surgical procedures, and public relations activities," Norma explains. "I use techniques such as photomicrography, photocopy, and preparation of slide series. My work is used for local training, national publication, documentation, and international conferences. I use a variety of special techniques and equipment in the medical work. I don't work with video or computer graphics, but more and more, medical photographers are making use of those techniques."

Norma recommends that photographers seeking work in the medical field should have experience and knowledge of operating cameras and related equipment and handling developing and printing processes and techniques, as well as a general knowledge of medicine and anatomy.

"Working for the federal government has been a great advantage for me," Norma says. "I started out in South Carolina, but my family is from western Massachusetts. Eventually, I was able to shift into a position at the Northampton hospital. That easy kind of switch, with no loss of salary, would have been much more difficult in private hospitals."

Working at a Military Base as a Civil Employee. Working for the federal government as a civil employee at a military base can be another path for a photography career. Harold Senn got his start by training at the air force photography school and spent eight years in the air force before leaving for civil service.

He then worked in industrial, public relations, and newspaper photography for the Charleston Naval Shipyard. His job was to "document the overhaul of navy ships; run a complete portrait studio; process and print color negatives, color slides, and black and whites; and do miscellaneous government paperwork."

Freelancing for Uncle Sam. Full-time photography positions with the federal government are hard to come by. Many more photography jobs in the federal government are filled on a temporary project basis. The research involved in working your way through the layers of agencies, departments, districts, and work units to the person who might be able and willing to hire you is extensive.

Ron Jameson hires freelance photographers to help track marine mammal migration patterns from the air. He advises that the freelancer should "find out which agencies might use photography in your region and go directly to them with inquiries." Because there isn't one clearinghouse you can go to, you have to do the basic research yourself to make your name and your abilities known. Then if someone on the inside likes your work, that person can help you wade through the bureaucratic procedures for hiring.

The Search for Opportunities

Searching for available jobs has become a great deal easier, thanks to the Internet. Two websites, in particular, are valuable tools: www.usajobs.opm.gov and www.fedjobs.com. In addition, every state's employment office or human resources division maintains information about local federal job openings and usually has an online database of all current listings.

Larger agencies such as the Forest Service, the Bureau of Indian Affairs, the Department of Fish and Wildlife, the Bureau of Land Management, and the National Biological Survey (there are many more), all contract out for photography on a project basis as needed, although some departments within the larger agencies may employ photographers on staff. *The Directory of Federal Government Procurement Offices* covers regional branches of agencies that buy products or hire services from outside the government.

Federal Career Opportunities is a biweekly bulletin that lists job openings by series and pay classification number, job title, and location. It is not an exhaustive listing—some jobs exist in some departments that may not be listed—but it does include many job openings. Subscriptions to this publication, both hard copy and online, are available at www.fedjobs.com or from Federal Research Service, P.O. Box 1708, Annandale, VA 22033. Most agency offices have copies of the bulletin as well. The same company provides the How to Get a Federal Job and Federal Application Forms Kit. Applying for a federal job is a three-step process. The first step is to use any of the automated components of the Federal Employment Information System, also known as USAJOBS, to find a job opening that interests you. The system provides an official website (www.usajobs.opm.gov), which gives you access to current listings as well as a means of obtaining the vacancy announcement. The vacancy announcement is an important source of information about the job itself, as well as closing and deadline dates for application, whether you must take a written test, education requirements, duty location, salary, and so on.

When it comes time to apply, you need to follow the application instructions listed on the vacancy announcement. Most jobs allow you to apply with a resume, or you may choose to fill out the standard application form OF-612, which can be downloaded from the website. Jobs with unique requirements often specify additional forms. Whatever application method you use, it is essential to include the following information:

- Announcement number, title, and grade
- Personal information, including full name, address, day and evening phone numbers, social security number, citizenship, veteran's preference (if you are a veteran), and highest federal civilian grade held
- Education, including the name, city, and state of your high school and college or university, along with majors and type and year of any degrees received (if no degree, show total credits earned and indicate semester or quarter hours)
- Work experience, including job title, duties, and accomplishments for each employer; employer's name, city, and state; supervisor's name and phone number; starting and ending dates (month and year is fine); whether the job

was full- or part-time (number of hours per week); and whether your current supervisor may be contacted

- Other qualifications, including job-related workshops or training courses (title and year) and job-related skills, certificates, licenses, honors, awards, or special accomplishments

Military Photography

Careers in military photography offer some distinct advantages—training, apprenticeship, potential travel. While the pay scales may seem low (enlisted recruits start at $12,514 per year), consider that the job includes housing, food, and health benefits, as well as educational training and opportunities for earning a college degree.

In the military, jobs are divided between officers and enlisted people. Many more possibilities exist for enlisted people interested in photography. As an officer, you would more likely be supervising photographers than shooting photographs, and there are no guarantees for officers that photography would be involved in their jobs.

If you enlist, on the other hand, you can find out about photography job availability and sign a contract for a specific position. Conditions in the four branches of the military (army, navy, air force, marines) change rapidly and are affected greatly in times of economic cutbacks, so research the possibilities thoroughly and carefully. And remember, joining the military is a serious decision. The contract is binding, and if you are assigned as a combat photographer you would be required to fight if the need arose.

Many photographers have gotten their starts in the military and praise the fine training available. The military has a need for many types of photography. A good place to begin your research if you are interested in a military career is with your local recruiting offices. They can provide information about the opportunities for training and work that currently exist in each of the branches of the service.

Photography Jobs in State and Local Government

Like the federal government, state and local governments use photography in countless ways. Finding out about these jobs means wending your way through less centralized but sometimes equally baffling bureaucracies than the federal government's. Your research skills will be well exercised as you look for possibilities within local and state governments, both as an in-house and a freelance photographer. Here are some suggestions for where to look:

- State colleges, universities, and community colleges—with professors, printing departments, science departments, public relations offices, or recruitment offices
- State agencies such as agriculture, fish and wildlife, transportation, forestry, natural resources, governor's office, tourist bureau, or human services
- County governments
- City and local governments

Your local state employment division is a good place to start to identify state or local positions that may be open. Full-time positions for photographers are rare. There may be one agency with a complete photo lab that services much of the statewide need for photographic services. In Arizona, for example, the state's Department of Photography operates a huge lab and provides services for all state agencies. By contrast, the Oregon Department of Forestry employs its own photographic technician who takes the work of aerial photographers and others and prepares the photos for use in cartography and publications.

The Range of Opportunity

Photography is an essential tool for state and local governments. Images are needed to advertise the state, to document government construction projects, and to explain natural resource problems to the public. Sometimes photographic support is needed in the scientific agencies to aid in research. Photographers are needed to provide images of evidence in county and local sheriff and police departments. Some examples of specialized government needs for photography follow.

Crime and Forensics Photography. To a large degree, the public image of a forensics photographer is overdramatized. Yes, your job may involve shooting at the scene of a crime. But in reality, the bulk of a forensics photographer's work involves slow, careful, accurate documentation of evidence. That means plenty of time in the lab taking pictures of bullets, documents, and weapons. It also means taking mug shots and photographs for police lineups as well as public relations photos and officer portraits.

The following list comes from a recent job description for the Las Vegas Metropolitan Police Department. The job is for a photo technician and pays between $2,099 and $3,106 monthly. The definition and essential functions of the job are as follows:

- Provide photographic support to LVMPD and neighboring police agencies; operate and maintain complex photographic equipment; and perform a variety of tasks relative to assigned areas of responsibility.
- Process and print black-and-white and color prints and proofs manually or using photographic processing equipment.
- Mix photographic chemicals; monitor and fill chemical tanks; use proper safety precautions.
- Cut, print, and package mug photos and proofs.
- Pull negatives and file accordingly.
- Cross reference negatives to assure correct numerical identification.
- Take photographs for police lineups, public relations, and portraits for LVMPD use.
- Make minor repairs and maintain photographic equipment; program printers as appropriate.

- Operate copy camera.
- Serve as lab receptionist.
- Stay abreast of new trends and innovations in photography.
- Fill in during supervisor's absence.

State police forces, county sheriff's offices, metropolitan police departments, and most medium-sized police departments support photography units of varying sizes, and both still and video photography skills are needed. A civil service examination is usually the basis for getting the job. An associate's degree in technical or commercial photography or two to three years of experience are standard entry-level job requirements. The pay ranges from $25,000 to start up to $55,000 for senior photographers.

Surveillance Photography. Many photographers are employed with police and investigative agencies to be part of surveillance operations. The Federal Bureau of Investigation, the Central Intelligence Agency, and state police departments all have photography units, but entering this field of employment requires that you first be either an agent or an officer with the organization. The role as police officer or investigator or agent comes first; the photography is a tool in the performance of the job. Salaries start between $23,790 and $31,410 for police officers.

Fire Photography. Like forensics photographers, fire photographers are often on the scene after the fire is put out, gathering evidence that might help understand the cause of the fire or solve arson cases. They are also involved with documenting firefighting efforts during a fire. Such documentation is often used for training purposes as well as public relations. Fire photographers wear protective clothing and use specially equipped cameras when covering a fire. Digital cameras are becoming the predominant choice for both still and video photography of fire events because they are less expensive than the cameras that protect film from extreme heat.

Both still and video cameras are used in fire photography, and depending on the size of the photography unit, you may be responsible for both. Fire photographers usually come to the position from the ranks of experienced firefighters. They are responsible for public relations photos as well as photo processing, if a lab exists on-site.

The pay scale for fire photographers is equivalent to firefighters' salary levels, which are established by local governments, and ranges from $23,000 to $48,000.

State Photo Services. Orrin Russie works as coordinator of a photo imaging services lab that serves state agencies from within a state agency. The lab is the only large in-house service in the state. He and four other photographers, all with at least fifteen years of experience, produce documentary videos for educational and training purposes and shoot, develop, and process still photos.

The lab does work for state departments, including the Justice Department, the Governor's Office, the Department of Insurance and Finance, and the Department of Human Resources. They do their own aerial photography to document all land acquisitions and surveys. If their projects require photogrammetric data, they contract with a private company that has the proper equipment.

Still images shot by the lab are used in several in-house publications for press releases and annual reports, as well as a selection of scenic photos that anyone can purchase. Photos also serve as documentation of public works projects, such as highway and bridge construction, and as documentation for legal purposes.

Groups within state agencies schedule portrait sittings as well. Sometimes Orrin travels to the agencies for portrait sittings or to photograph an event. And there's always copy work needed to get a publication ready to be printed.

State Colleges and Universities. Large universities and colleges within each state system of higher education often have their own photo services departments, and sometimes individual divisions or units will have a separate lab with a staff of photographers and photo technicians. Oregon State University, for example, has one full-time photographer in University Publications and three full-time photographers in Communications Media Services. The Forest Research Lab employs another full-time photographer, and Agricultural, Extension, and Sea Grant Communications Departments have both still and video photographers on staff.

Part Photographer, Part Writer

If you are willing for photography to be only a part of your job description, you may find more possibilities open to you. Pat Ray, information supervisor for the Oregon Department of Fish and Wildlife, notes that his position with the state is less than half-time photography—closer to 20 percent. In fact, there are no positions within the ODFW for full-time photographers, which is the biggest disadvantage for the aspiring natural resources photographer, according to Pat.

"A very common quality among natural resources agencies is a dedication to the resource," according to Pat; so if your passion is natural resources, a job that combines photography with writing and editing might be appealing. In his position, Pat researches and writes about various facets of fish and wildlife management, works on the radio show that he puts together with a coworker, produces news releases that can include photographs from the field, deals with the media, or is out in the field covering stories or projects. The photography he does is used in several in-house publications, slide shows, and presentations. For such a writing-editing-photography position, the salary range is currently $22,921 to $43,484. Entry-level salaries for photographers with state government agencies range from $19,389 to $23,219, which varies according to the region and the photographer's education and experience.

Advice from a Government Photographer

Obtaining government jobs is highly competitive. At Orrin Russie's lab, budgets are so tight that he can't hire assistants or freelancers, though he sometimes uses student interns.

Orrin's advice to the aspiring photographer is to remember that there are "not many jobs for professional photographers with a good wage—period. The competition is keen." You have to be in the right place at the right time, Orrin advises, to find a position with the state. You must also be well trained. And any experience you can get—as an intern, volunteer, or freelancer—will give you an edge.

For More Information

Organizations
Association of Federal Photographers
P.O. Box 46097
Washington, DC 20050

Association of Investigative Photographers
P.O. Box 479
Charles Town, WV 25414

Evidence Photographers International Council
600 Main Street
Honesdale, PA 18431
www.epic-photo.org

International Fire Photographers Association
P.O. Box 8337
Rolling Meadows, IL 60008
www.firephotographers.com/ifpa

Books
The Implementation of Digital Photography in Law Enforcement & Government: An Overview Guide, by Craig A. Coppock et al. Charles C. Thomas Publisher, Limited.
Opportunities in Military Careers: A Guide to Military Occupations and Selected Military Career Paths, by Adrian A. Paradis. McGraw-Hill.

CHAPTER TEN

The World at Work

Corporate and Industrial Photography

When you think of industrial photography, do you imagine big machinery and manufacturing plants, assembly lines, arc welders, and giant furnaces? Although industrial photography indeed encompasses manufacturing plants, it also covers a wide range of subjects, from executive portraiture in twenty-fifth-floor offices to modern-day mining operations at two hundred feet beneath the earth's surface, from panoramic shots of a four-hundred-acre industrial park to extreme close-ups of a tiny U-joint at an airplane repair facility.

Industrial photography involves photographing the people, equipment, machinery, and work of the nation's builders, manufacturers, engineers, agriculturists, and developers. From the publications department of a major computer manufacturer to the offices of a Fortune 500 company, industrial photography offers both challenges and rewards for talented photographers.

Many industrial photographers freelance, although this field is often defined as in-house photography. Both kinds of opportunities exist within the field, and the earning potential can be the same for the entrepreneurial freelancer as for the corporate department head. Some globe-trotting industrial photographers working either on staff or under contract for multinational corporations travel from site to site documenting the work of the corporation for annual reports, brochures, company recruitment publications, or press releases destined for the business pages of major newspapers or industry trade publications.

Problems of Industrial Photography

Industrial photography offers some tough challenges to creative photographers. Much of your time is spent working to get good photographs of objects that have little visual interest or appeal in settings that may be colorless and dim or with subjects who may not be comfortable being photographed. Such circumstances can be enough to scare off the most dedicated of photographers. If you can consistently achieve good results in such situations, you're going to be in great demand as an industrial photographer!

Identification and communication are the central facets of industrial and corporate photography. The industrial photographer needs to understand the purpose of the photographs, the message they will be used to convey, and the audience who will receive the photographs as part of a larger communication.

The photographer responsible for photographing employees for the in-house newsletter should be able to approach each situation with a fresh eye in order to avoid a stale sameness in the publication's look. Often these publications have worldwide distribution to a circulation list larger than some daily newspapers.

A more practical consideration involves safety. Sometimes the industrial photographer is working in potentially dangerous situations with heavy equipment, high-voltage electricity, molten metal, or scaffolding hanging from I-beams forty floors up. Coordinating lighting and its accompanying cords and battery packs in these situations can be hazardous both for the photographer and the subjects. It's essential to have training in safety procedures and to get full information about each situation before you go in to shoot.

Advice from Industrial Photographers

Walter Farrell has worked as an industrial photographer for a mining company in Nevada. His work has taken him to mining operations in Africa, England, France, and South America. On the home front, he spends his time both in the studio shooting portraits of company executives, still lifes of raw and processed ore samples, and staged photo illustrations of engineering and chemical processes. After eighteen years, he offers some sage advice.

"When you're working on location, do as much research as you can about the job before you arrive," he advises. "If you will be working with people, make sure they know you are coming and are ready to cooperate. They may have a different understanding than you do about the project. Find out what you can about the setting, the lighting needs, and the availability of electricity. Develop a plan for solving the problems presented by the assignment, and then make a backup plan."

Walter works with an assistant if the situation is complex or potentially hazardous. He feels that having an extra pair of eyes keeping track of all the variables can be well worth the expense of hiring a freelance assistant.

Corporate photographer Tamlin Gregory works for a major food-processing company in Iowa. She handles virtually all photography needs for the company, including advertising, public relations, quarterly and annual reports, the staff newsletter, and product packaging photos.

"It's a real whirlwind, but I love the variety," she says. "And there's a surprising amount of creative freedom, when you think of the subject matter. Canned corn isn't exactly my ideal subject matter, but you'd be surprised the amount of fun you can have setting up a still life that communicates something more than corn kernels in a can."

Tamlin often hires freelance photographers and assistants, especially for working in the field. Her annual and quarterly report photographs typically involve getting good agricultural photos of corporate farming operations, and sometimes her schedule doesn't allow her to be away from the central studio when the corn is ripe and ready for harvest.

"I'd advise beginners to seek out freelancing and assisting opportunities," Tamlin adds. "That's how I got my start, and the experience I gained was invaluable. I'm still using the tips I learned from the first photographer I assisted. He was a terrific mentor."

What You Need to Know

Because industrial photography can be expensive for the client—it may involve machinery shutdown or a halt in productivity among employees who are subjects—companies usually will not hire someone who doesn't have a strong reputation. Your portfolio needs to reflect a high degree of expertise in photography itself, as well as a creative approach to capturing often prosaic images in an appealing, interesting light.

Your skills as a photographer need to be varied. You might need to photograph inside a large warehouse, at a banquet for corporate stockholders, or in a studio situation with a still-life setup. Photographers specializing in only one of these areas most likely work independently. Staff photographers have to do it all.

Practical experience, preferably with an experienced industrial photographer, is the only way to get your start in this highly competitive field. Working as a freelance assistant for a variety of independent corporate photographers can provide a broad range of experience in different situations and for different types of industrial clients.

A degree from a respected school of photography gives you the background you need to be hired as an assistant by an experienced professional. Although a degree often isn't required, the experience you gain in all aspects of technical expertise will pay off, and it will give you an advantage over photographers without college experience. Corporate and industrial photography demands much more than just pictures. The images must represent the company and its products at their best. To achieve this the photographer must have exceptional technical fluency and creativity.

Specialty Areas in Industrial and Corporate Photography

When we think of corporate or industrial photography, it's easy to limit our thinking to Fortune 500 companies or auto manufacturers in Detroit. The field is much broader, including many areas of photography that have applications in other fields as well.

Industrial photographers who work on staff tend to be generalists, available to handle the photographic needs of a variety of corporate divisions. The legal department might need photographs of faulty equipment; the security division might need you to photograph all staff people for identification badges; the marketing department might need a special product photograph for a trade show poster. In some cases, the industrial or corporate staff photographer must also operate or supervise a darkroom lab on-site.

What follows are a few of the specialty areas of industrial and corporate photography. The list is not all-inclusive; virtually any industry could form the basis of a specialty.

Agricultural Photography
The agricultural photographer spends much of the time out in the field, whether it's a field of wheat in Nebraska, sugar cane in the Philippines, coffee trees in Colombia, or pineapple in Hawaii. Photographs of crops, insects, farm implements, planting and harvesting methods, soils, and damaged crops are all subject matter for agricultural photography.

Not all the time is spent outdoors, however. Photographs of laboratory operations and processing plants or studio still-life and photo-illustration shots for educational purposes form other important aspects of the agricultural photographer's work.

Annual Reports
Many corporate or industrial photographers specialize in taking photographs for annual reports, those slick publications designed to impress stockholders with the corporation's stability and achievements in the previous year. Any corporation or organization with public stock on the market must by law produce an annual report to its stockholders. For many corporations, the annual report becomes a major promotional tool to encourage more confident investment. Therefore, companies set aside significant budget resources for the preparation of this document.

The subject matter in annual reports varies widely. What the annual report photographer offers is a certain cachet or sense of style that will provide the corporation with a "look" to appeal to its shareholders. Annual report photos are prepared by either staff or independent photographers.

Architectural Photography

Architectural firms, construction companies, realtors, and businesses or industries that commission such firms are likely clients for architectural photography. Images of buildings, both exterior and interior, are also frequently used in corporate annual reports.

Architectural photographers record everything from the initial scale models created by the architects to the finished realization of the design once the structure is completed. Architectural photographs are used by architects to enter national and international contests, to submit to trade publications, and to provide visual portfolios to prospective clients.

Related specialties include construction and interior design photography. While the architectural photographer is interested primarily in a building's aesthetic elements, construction photographs provide an important record of building methods and procedures for construction corporations.

The interior photographer works with completed interiors for the same clients but with an eye toward capturing the design and details of a room. Hotels, restaurants, furniture manufacturers, architects, interior design companies, and corporations with expensive offices or public areas are all potential clients.

Audiovisual Presentations

Many organizations—both public and private, profit and non-profit—have a need to communicate both with images and spoken information to an audience, a classroom, or on individual monitors. Making these audiovisual presentations is a major career field in itself, but because of its close relationship to photography, and the opportunities this field presents to photographers, it's appropriately included here.

Audiovisual slide presentations, filmstrips, and videos are all part of the medium, and each can involve photography. Because of the extensive use of audiovisual materials in education, many college students become familiar with the medium, perhaps working in an on-campus AV lab.

Insurance Photography
Many corporations or businesses with significant resources tied up in expensive equipment will maintain a photographic record of acquisitions. Insurance companies also often want to document the condition of property they will be insuring or damages that have occurred to insured property. Only the largest corporations or insurance companies have on-staff photographers. Insurance photography is primarily a freelance occupation.

Legal Photography
Although the age of digital computers and easy, seamless manipulation of images has cast doubt on photographs as reliable evidence, this is still an area in which corporate or industrial photographers can find opportunities. Corporations with the potential for liability claims may need photographic documentation for presentation to insurance companies or attorneys. Like insurance photography, this is an area with opportunity primarily for freelance photographers, but it carries an extra demand that the photographer have a strong reputation for honesty and reliability.

Public Relations Photography
While closely related to advertising, public relations involves more than just the product or service—it involves the entire company. Public relations activities involve in-house newsletters, press releases being sent to newspapers and trade magazines, and ongoing press relations. Photographers in public relations work have a specific communications purpose beyond imparting information. The PR photograph involves a "spin" or "slant" that presents the company or people who work for the company in a positive light.

Opportunities exist for staff and freelance photography with any corporation or organization, such as a university, hospital, charitable organization, or PR firm. Public relations firms, like advertising agencies, provide services to organizations that don't have their own PR departments.

Product Photography

Every manufacturer, producer, retailer, designer, and purveyor of goods or services needs to make the public aware of the product being offered for sale. Photography provides the visual component of that message. While product photography is primarily an advertising or commercial function, industrial and corporate photographers are frequently called upon to photograph the computers, cars, machine parts, boxer shorts, bean sprouts, or xylophones their companies create.

The uses of product photography are many. A product that has recently been developed must be patented to protect it from appropriation by another manufacturer. To apply to the U.S. Patent Office, a manufacturer must send photographs documenting the specific details of the product. Once patented, the product is prepared for marketing. Artistic or aesthetically pleasing photographs are taken for advertising and promotional purposes. Press packages are put together to send to trade publications to announce the new product, complete with photographs to be reproduced in the magazines.

Photographic Administration

The larger the corporation, the greater and more varied the needs for photography. In these cases, the department of photography might include twenty or more staff members, including darkroom workers and freelancers hired to pick up the extra work. The photographic administrator is most likely responsible for all photography operations, including processing-lab workers, darkroom printers, and photographers.

Promotions to administration positions almost always come from within the organization, whether it's a government agency or an industrial giant. A college degree is generally required for advancement to this level, though a demonstrated ability for management and organization will be most significant. The administrator might be responsible for a sizable budget, so course work in business procedures and administration can be helpful.

Freelance Industrial Photography

There is room for both freelancers and staff photographers in the industrial photography field, and sometimes companies with in-house photographers hire freelancers as well. Often corporate and industrial photographers work with agents or photographer's representatives, especially if they are in one of the larger markets such as New York, Philadelphia, Chicago, or Detroit.

The Daily Routine

Like most other areas of photography, a daily routine is a contradiction in terms for the industrial or corporate photographer. Very little in this business can be called routine. One day you'll be photographing the CEO for the annual report, the next you'll be on a plane to cover an accident at the company's plant in Mexico. You might photograph a new product in the studio, a worker on the assembly line, a farmer tilling a field of wheat, or a wildcatter on the deck of an oil rig. And that might all be for the same company. Major corporations often have multiple investments that cross over industry lines and national borders.

Lewis Nelson, who owns a small industrial and scientific studio in Oregon, started his business after finishing an exciting job shooting a slide presentation for the state of Washington. Because he was in graduate school, he knew the research scientists who became his first clients. From this beginning, he slowly built a client base among local industries and corporations.

Lewis photographs small products or inventions for manufacturing companies throughout the state. Primarily he takes the photos in his studio, but occasionally he sets up a shoot on location in the plant. One such project involved documenting the development and installation of a recycling system at a pulp and paper mill.

Income Potential

The median annual earnings of salaried industrial photographers in 2000 was $22,300, with the middle 50 percent earning between $16,700 and $33,020. Starting salaries for working in the darkroom of a large corporation department average $14,000 to $17,000. The darkroom can serve as a good starting position. You may be asked to take some of the in-house photographs needed for the company newsletter, for example.

Photographic administrators earn between $29,124 and $84,473, depending on the geographic region and the size of the organization.

About eight hundred thousand people are employed in the audiovisual industry, which has an average salary of $33,010. An audiovisual specialist on staff receives a salary ranging from a low of $19,178 to a high of $43,858. A specialist operating an independent AV company can earn in excess of $100,000 per year, especially when working with large corporate or industrial clients. For freelancers, *Photographer's Market* listings indicate potential audiovisual clients, as well as other business and corporate clients willing to look at the work of new talent.

The freelancer's income is based primarily on the amount of energy and time spent developing a base of clients, as well as the photography budgets of the clients themselves. Rates vary from $200 to $1,600 per day for corporate photography.

The clients paying the highest rates hire only the best, most innovative corporate photographers to work on annual reports for the world's richest corporations. But with a strong portfolio, technical expertise, experience, and a reputation for creativity and style behind you, you can begin to attract offers from clients willing to pay day rates of $1,500 or better.

For More Information

Organizations
International Industrial Photographers Association
Fur Photography
Orteliusdreef 10
2661 RL Bergschenhoek
The Netherlands
www.furphoto.net/iipa.htm

Books
Corporate and Location Photography, by Gary Gladstone. The
   Company.
How to Photograph Buildings and Interiors, by Gerry Kopelow.
   Princeton Architectural Press.

Periodicals
AV Video and Multimedia Producer
Knowledge Industry Publications Incorporated
701 Westchester Avenue
White Plains, NY 10604

Industrial Photography
Cygnus Publishing
P.O. Box 460
Fort Atkinson, WI 53538
   (Monthly magazine for industrial photographers.)

CHAPTER ELEVEN

The Fantastic Voyage

Scientific and Medical Photography

D o you have a scientific mind? Are you curious about the astounding new technologies affecting medical practices and scientific research? If you have a fascination with and knowledge of human anatomy, biology, botany, the laws of physics, space research, or any number of areas in science and medicine, a career in scientific photography may be just where you're heading.

Scientific Photography

Photography's ability to detect and to document what the human eye cannot see has always made it an important tool for scientists. In fact, for many years photography courses at colleges and universities were offered through the science department because photography itself was considered a science.

The techniques of extreme close-up or magnification photography (photomacrography); microprojection photography of minute objects (photomicrography); and the making of minute photographs of large objects (microphotography) are at the core of the photography used for scientific application.

Photomacrography and photomicrography can provide lasting records for the study of the process of a dragonfly's transition from a nymphal shell or the moment an egg is fertilized. Microphotography is used in microchip technology, in which large but intricate drawings are photographed and reduced to tiny chips, then the metals used in processing settle along the now-minute drawn lines and become conductors of electronic impulses.

High-speed or time-lapse photography provides data that allow a zoologist to study the motions and physiology of a bat or aid an astronomer in gathering data about the movements of satellites around a distant star.

Many technical applications of photography—optics and photogrammetry, for example—require specialized equipment and training and are performed by scientists or technicians rather than photographers. Some of the uses of photographic techniques and principles in the sciences may not look like photography at all to a shutterbug. And, in fact, scientists and engineers often take their own scientific photographs, making the need for a dedicated photographer less common than in some other fields.

But don't abandon the idea just yet. Not only are some of these techniques accessible to even the amateur photographer, but there is photographic work for the scientifically minded shutterbug who doesn't want to be an astronomer or physician or engineer. Photographers are needed to provide the images necessary to represent ideas and the results of experimentation; to provide images for press releases, newsletters, annual reports, and brochures; and to perform the variety of general photography needed in many scientific fields.

The Range of Opportunity

Photography opportunities in the science fields range from highly technical to very general. A freelance photographer could build a small business on producing images for research scientists. A scientifically minded photo expert could become involved in research and development of lenses and equipment in the optics field. A photographer could become an expert in photomicrography in a teaching hospital, taking pictures through a microscope. What follows are some examples of the many photography-related careers in the world of science.

Instrumentation Photography. Most commonly associated with the military, where much of the research for space and defense application is done, this field is part of the engineering research process. Engineers need high-speed photographs to assist in the study and development of rockets, missiles, and anything that moves through space.

Instrumentation photographers may find themselves working on the research and development of instrumentation photographic systems. They may work on problem solving for specific needs, such as measuring the trajectory of a rocket or the detonation of a weapon.

Photogrammetry. Photogrammetry, the art of measuring and interpreting vertical aerial photographs for making maps, is a photography-related career area that has been especially affected by computer technology, to the point of completely redefining the job. Technologies such as Global Positioning System (GPS) and Geographic Information Systems (GIS)—computerized databases of spatial data—are changing the field.

It is possible to gain experience as a cartographer or technician without an undergraduate degree, but more and more often, particularly with the changes in the field related to systems like GIS, photogrammetrists have bachelor's degrees in engineering, computer science, geography, or a physical science. Used primarily for map making and defense purposes, photogrammetry also has some biomedical applications, such as the measurement of a facial pattern before orthodontic treatment.

Optics. The optics field is a highly technical engineering field. It involves various photography-related careers ranging from technicians who shape lenses and optical elements using hand-operated grinding and polishing equipment to technicians who operate cameras in the lab to research-and-development technicians and scientists. Optics technicians often graduate from two-year training programs, gaining experience in various parts of the field through internships and training offered through professional associations.

The optics field is predominantly applied in space and weapons programs, but it is also vital in the research, development, and manufacture of cameras, binoculars, telescopes, and other optical devices.

Aerial Photography. In the biological and natural resource sciences, photography is an important tool for aiding scientists in study. Photography is used to document events in the natural world, to record habitat for a certain species or for an entire ecosystem, to document population in an area, and to illustrate presentations and reports. Scientists usually take their own pictures in the field, but sometimes work is contracted out. Special color infrared photos detect vegetation at small scales and enable aerial photographers to track changes in vegetation from environmental influences over time. Aerial photography is used in many industries as well as ecosystem, agriculture, wildlife, and forest management. As an aerial photographer, you are at an advantage if you are also a pilot. Most aerial photographers do fly; if you don't, you'll need to develop a working relationship with a pilot.

Underwater Photography. Oceanographers and marine biologists work with photographers at marine laboratories and research stations around the world. Photographers might also work aboard research vessels such as those operated by the famous Cousteau Society. Research employment is primarily through universities, but private corporations, particularly those involved with offshore oil or other resources, also hire photographers to document underwater terrain, wave action, or evidence of geothermal activity. Environmental agencies involved with the protection of endangered species or habitats hire photographers to document conditions injurious to fish or wildlife.

An underwater or oceanographic photographer will need to be a skilled scuba diver with a thorough understanding of the safety issues, as well as the technical demands, of photographing underwater. Special equipment is also essential.

Other Specialty Fields and Opportunities. Photographers with special backgrounds in archaeology, botany, plant pathology,

entomology, zoology—virtually any field of scientific endeavor—
have opportunities for working in research situations, both on
staff and freelance. Places of employment include the following:

- Government agencies
- Hospitals
- Manufacturing companies
- Museums of science and industry
- Research and development departments of major
  corporations
- Research organizations and associations
- Research stations
- Scientific laboratories
- Universities

Photographer as Lab Assistant

Andy Baird stumbled into a career in scientific photography when
he got his first job in the psychology lab at Princeton University.
He learned to implant miniature electrodes into rat brains with
high precision and later to dissect the preserved brains for micro-
scopic examination. He took pictures throughout the procedure,
then created an animated film showing the action of neurotrans-
mitter hormones at the nerve synapse in a symbolic form that
made the complex biochemistry easy to grasp visually.

He went on to work as a lab technician at the university's Audi-
tory Research Lab. "I again photographed everything in sight,
from the staff to the bats and lizards, which were the subjects of
our research on hearing," Andy recalls. "When one scientist
obtained a small grant from the National Geographic Society to
go to Costa Rica and study pollinating bats and their ecosystems,
I went along as a field assistant and, of course, photographer. I can
tell you that nothing will get your luggage through customs faster
than having a large, brilliant orange sticker that says, 'Camera
Equipment/National Geographic Society'!"

Freelancing

For those shutterbugs who want to remain photographers first and scientists second, one possibility is freelancing for scientists. The work involved in such a venture could range from photographing petri dish experiments for a graduate research project to completing aerial photography for a natural resource agency.

Susan Peters, who works for an industrial, commercial, and scientific photography service in Corvallis, Oregon, photographs specimens for research scientists at the local university. Most often, she photographs bacteria, petri dishes, and autoradiograms—a technique using radioactive materials to separate bacteria and DNA, RNA, and proteins that are grown on lab gels. Another large part of her work involves slide copying.

The nature of her work is changing, in part because computer technology has become so accessible to scientists, making it possible for them to generate their own images and graphs from personal computers. But the abundance of copy work and slide making has remained fairly consistent. The work is contracted to Susan at $85 per hour; of course, rates vary depending on locale and demand, and a staff person would make much less per hour.

From Pathology to Stock Photography

Another option if you are fascinated with taking biological or medical photos is to sell your photography to textbook companies, scientific magazines, and pharmaceutical companies. Henry M. Schleichkorn began his photography career early. "Since the age of seven, I have had an undeniable passion for photography," he recalls. "By the time I was fifteen, there was no turning back; I was shooting portraiture, nature photography, and journalism photography professionally. We all knew school would have to center around photography.

"After graduating from the State University of New York at Farmingdale with an A.A.S. degree in photographic technology, I studied medical photography with Bruce Grant, Bill DuBois, and Nile Root at the Rochester Institute of Technology, receiving my B.S. in biomedical photographic communications in 1982.

"Straight out of RIT I was hired by Dr. Leon LeBeau as the scientific photographer for the Department of Pathology at the University of Illinois Medical Center. In 1983, I was board certified as a Registered Biological Photographer (RBP) by the Biological Photographic Association (now known as the BioCommunications Association).

"I truly feel RIT gave me the background and, more importantly, confidence, to chase a dream by starting my own business. I started Custom Medical Stock Photo, Inc. CMSP has grown into an international stock photo company with medical and scientific images being represented by agencies in more than forty countries worldwide. With the explosion of Internet use, marketing, selling, and delivering images online has helped CMSP become a leader in medical and scientific stock photography and illustration. Our growth has been unbelievable. We represent the creative works of more than three hundred contributors. We are constantly reviewing portfolios and looking for new images that help enhance and educate today's written word.

"Our latest project is designed to help educate students worldwide. It is a database of fifty thousand images, which will be available to students, lecturers, and educators, online at www.educationalpictures.com.

"I enjoy the photography and creative end of life and of business," Henry says. "I create images every day. I love seeing my images in magazines, textbooks, and advertisements. At times, my family helps out by modeling. In fact, my youngest son, Avery, appeared on the cover of *My Weekly Reader* magazine recently."

Chapter 6 includes more information about the stock photography business.

Education, Outlook, and Earnings

Several colleges and universities offer specific programs in scientific and biomedical photography. Instruction emphasizes taking a scientific approach to problem solving. Areas of concentration include patient photography, medical documentation, public relations, lighting for studio and location photography, copy photography, macrophotography, radiograph reproduction photomicrography, and video and audiovisual presentation. A two-year technical degree is the minimum requirement for most staff positions, but a four-year degree with scientific course work in addition to the photography training will be a significant advantage.

Science and technology will continue to become more important and more integrated into society in the future. However, as technology becomes more advanced, computer capabilities grow, and the applications for computerized photographic techniques become more user friendly, straightforward photography jobs in the sciences may become tougher to find. Scientists have always taken pictures as part of their research, and technologies that are more accessible to the nonprofessional photographer are increasingly important for the scientist to master.

A scientific photographer with a strong background in science and photography could obtain a staff position at a university or corporate research department with a salary ranging from $28,275 to $43,586 per year with a median of $35,139. According to the *Occupational Outlook Handbook*, median annual earnings of photogrammetrists in 2000 were $39,410, with the middle 50 percent earning between $29,200 and $51,930. The lowest 10 percent earned less than $23,560, and the highest 10 percent earned more than $64,780.

Medical Photography

Within the medical profession, there is a great need for photographs, from general photography of the places, events, and staff personalities for public relations use to patient and specimen photography for diagnosis and disease research. Taking photographs for diagnostic or investigative purposes often involves both highly specialized equipment and extensive training.

An in-house photographer or illustration department is common in larger hospitals and teaching hospitals. Sometimes technical photography is performed as one duty of a technician or nurse or even surgeon rather than a designated photographer. Highly specialized photographic needs must be met by technicians trained in the scientific processes. Medical photographers usually have knowledge of human anatomy, physiology, and surgical procedures.

According to a personnel officer at a small private hospital in Oregon, most small hospitals don't have enough funds to employ a photographer. In this case, a department manager who is also an amateur photographer does the hospital's in-house photography. And physicians in the operating room take care of their own photography with the help of fixed equipment. Hospitals without staff photographers may need to hire out photographic work.

Physicians and technicians use technical photographic techniques in their diagnoses and research. Gastroendoscopes photograph the inside of the stomach and esophagus. Ophthalmic medicine applies photographic techniques in its study of the eye, for both observation and diagnosis. X-ray photography involves specialized training and equipment for technicians and is a part of virtually every hospital, clinic, and laboratory.

Digital Future

Digital technology has had major impact on medical applications. Electronic imaging systems are being refined for use in plastic surgery, allowing the physician to apply enhancements and alterations of a patient's facial features on screen, providing a "preview" before actually beginning surgery.

Medical schools, too, have developed computer programs as educational techniques, such as a gross anatomy dissector that simulates step-by-step dissection procedures and includes digitized photographs that are so realistic that one medical student commented, "For some people, the dissector was so real and complete that they sometimes didn't have to come to lab."

The Workday

Jess Lopatynski worked as a medical photographer for ten years at a children's hospital. A former instructor at Brooks Institute of Photography in California recommended that he apply for the position of staff medical photographer.

"As an in-house photographer, your day is a combination of the mundane and the interesting," Jess explains. "At one time, I did a study on blood flow using infrared photography for the Veterans Administration, but I also did my share of public relations photos and grip-and-grins. I might spend an hour in an operating room doing photos of a club foot correction on a child, then spend all afternoon copying x-rays to slides."

Jess's photo assignments came primarily from physicians at the hospital but also from administrative, nursing, and other specialized staff. He estimates that 10 percent of his work was studio work, 10 percent clinical, 20 percent clerical, 30 percent copy work, and the rest darkroom work.

Education, Outlook, and Earnings

Some medical photographers get involved in the field without specific medical training. Jess Lopatynski, for example, moved into medical photography from industrial photography—"from nuts and bolts to blood and guts," Jess laughs. Being a highly skilled photographer is enough, some say, for any photography job. Generally, however, it is advisable to gain at least a general background in the sciences and basic knowledge of human anatomy, surgical procedures, and medical practices. A four-year degree will give you a significant advantage in gaining a staff position and will increase your earnings potential. Brooks Institute of Photography and Rochester Institute of Technology are highly recommended training institutions for medical photographers. Course specialties at RIT's Biomedical Photography Communications program include electronic photography and video, magnification photography, ophthalmic photography, intermediate advertising, advanced AV production, nature instrumentation, holography, scanning electron microscopy, videotape production, advanced microscopy, and computer graphics. Certification is also highly recommended, especially if you hope to advance in your career.

Employment possibilities in medical photography include forensic labs, pharmaceutical companies, health care and medical research centers, ophthalmic practices, as well as law enforcement and military organizations.

The employment outlook for medical photography is good through 2010, according to the *Occupational Outlook Handbook*. The increase in population—and the aging of the population—means an increase in the number and size of hospitals, the primary employer of medical photographers. University hospitals are also excellent prospects for medical photographers because they combine documentation with training needs.

The salary for medical photographers on staff ranges from $28,275 to $43,000 and more. Positions at private teaching hospitals start slightly higher.

For More Information

Professional Associations

ASPRS: The Imaging and Geospatial Information Society
5410 Grosvenor Lane, Suite 210
Bethesda, MD 20814
www.asprs.org

BioCommunications Association
115 Stone Ridge Drive
Chapel Hill, NC 27514
www.bca.org

Ophthalmic Photographers' Society
3632 Blaine Avenue
St. Louis, MO 63110
www.opsweb.org

The Society for Imaging Science and Technology (IS&T)
7003 Kilworth Lane
Springfield, VA 22151
www.imaging.org

Periodicals

Journal of Electronic Imaging
The Society for Imaging Science and Technology
7003 Kilworth Lane
Springfield, VA 22151
www.imaging.org

> *(Copublished by the Society for Imaging Science and Technology and the International Society for Optical Engineering four times annually. Focuses on papers in all technology areas that make up the field of electronic imaging.)*

Journal of Imaging Science & Technology
The Society for Imaging Science and Technology
7003 Kilworth Lane
Springfield, VA 22151
www.imaging.org

> *(Bimonthly publication designed to provide the imaging community documentation of a broad range of research, development, and applications in imaging.)*

CHAPTER TWELVE

On Gallery Walls
Fine Art Photography

F ine art photography is an art medium that allows the photographer to create a visual representation of a personal vision or expression. The fine art photographer is bound by no limits of technology or medium, freely combining and experimenting to develop a unique aesthetic.

The acceptance of photography as a fine art medium has increased steadily since William Henry Fox Talbot published his photograph *The Open Door* in 1844. It has been acknowledged as the first photograph published solely for its aesthetic value. It wasn't until the 1890s that the first photography exhibit by a major art museum was mounted by the Royal Academy in Berlin. Today most museums of fine art have extensive collections of fine art photography, and fine art galleries increasingly number photographers among the artists they represent. The number of galleries dedicated to exhibiting photography also has increased.

While all this has been good news for fine art photographers, the reality is that it is still very difficult to make a living exclusively from fine art photography. Harrison Branch, a professor of art at Oregon State University, estimates that between 2 and 10 percent of those involved in fine art photography are able to make a living at it. "And that's being generous," he adds with a laugh.

Among the highly successful fine art photographers are the big names such as Annie Liebowitz, Edward Weston, Walker Evans, Duane Michals, or Herb Ritts. Their prints earn top dollar through galleries in New York and across the country. But developing that level of name recognition takes time, dedication, perseverance, and, foremost, a distinctive, original, and powerful personal style.

For many photographers, being able to engage in the creative side of their work is the reason they take wedding photographs or portraits or work day jobs as lab technicians. These other jobs keep food on the table; the fine art photography feeds the soul.

What It Takes

Creative photographers, says Harrison, don't need an academic degree, although as a university professor, he believes in the value of education—especially as a time to expand your creative vision while you have a built-in source of critical feedback. "What you really need is talent, and you need luck."

Luck comes with developing the gallery connections that get your work shown. "You have to find those who like your work, understand your work, and are willing to exhibit your work," Harrison explains. "You may be one of the world's greatest photographers, but if you don't have any gallery connections, your work never gets shown."

A Way of Seeing

The talent part of Harrison's formula, he says, has to come from within. "You must have some kind of imagination," he insists. "You have to have an eye. It's an old cliché, but it applies to photography the same way it applies to painting, printmaking, graphic design, or any other visual area. If you don't have an eye, you're just taking up space."

The "eye" involves the artist's way of seeing, the artist's approach to creating visual images. The elements of design—composition, light, texture, form, value—are all important, but to Harrison they are secondary to the artist's idea.

"You have to be able to make your photograph communicate something, some essential reason for existing besides just being a pretty picture. It should communicate something about what I know. It should enlighten me about something I don't know. You could be the world's greatest photographic technician, but if you have no sensitivity, no eye, it won't make your photographs exciting or moving. Technique alone does not make a photographer."

Another important learning tool involves looking at the work of others—reading books on photography, haunting art galleries and museums, browsing library bookshelves for art photography books. "Look at everyone and everything," Harrison advises. "Don't limit yourself by looking only at work by people you like. Look at work by people you don't like. Ask yourself, 'Why do I like this person?' and 'What is it about this work that I don't like?'"

An Ability to Solve Visual Problems

While a degree in photography isn't required, there's a great deal that can be learned in the classroom aside from technical knowledge. Good programs in photography help you learn how to approach taking pictures as a means of solving a visual problem.

"In school, assignments are given so that you can go out and challenge your imagination to see how inventive you can be," Harrison explains. "In the best situations, you're challenged not only by your professor but by your fellow students. Once you're out there in the world working on your own, you have to maintain that inventiveness, that sense of personal challenge."

Finding others to critique your work can be very useful, even to the professional photographer with years of experience. Joining a photography guild or association can provide that kind of help. "You can do nothing but benefit from having other people around to talk to about photography," Harrison says. "It's one of the best learning tools there is—having someone else's shoulder to cry on!"

The Determination to Keep Going

Perseverance and tough skin are also important attributes for a would-be successful fine art photographer. It takes a fair amount of gumption to walk into an art gallery and ask to show your work and then have to wait and watch while the gallery director looks through your portfolio. Perhaps a worse situation is waiting weeks after having dropped your portfolio by the gallery only to have it returned with a short form letter saying, "Thanks, but no thanks."

One photographer recalls showing his work to a gallery director in New York who fanned through the pages in about ten seconds, put them down on the table, and walked away without a word. That's the height of the rudeness you might encounter, but it's important to remember not to take it personally or let it stop you.

Harrison argues that the same is true for critiques from fellow photographers. "Take them with a grain of salt. They're part of a learning process, not personal attacks. They're meant to make you a better image maker."

Digital Fine Art Photography

In talking with fine art photographers, you'll find an entire range of reaction to the impact of digital photography on fine arts. Some are vehemently opposed to the manipulation that digital photography allows once the photograph has been taken. Others are gleefully pursuing the many creative doors the new technology has flung open. Jim Williams is a corporate photographer by day, a fine art photographer on his own time. At the office, he is very involved with the new technology, using it to enhance and manipulate images to create advertising and promotional products.

In his own work, however, he likes to keep the images raw. "Having worked with digital image manipulation daily for five years now, I've had a kind of backlash," Jim says. "My personal photography documents the lives and work of ballet dancers. Because ballet is a classical art, I used to work very hard at clean, uncluttered compositions—making sure the edges were straight, with no awkward corners or odd bits of scenery sticking in, no intrusive background elements. I've even tried taking flawed pictures and 'improving' them by erasing distractions, smoothing backgrounds, and so on. But I almost always found I liked the original image better. I'm starting to enjoy flaunting the photographic nature of my pictures, using their imperfections as a badge of unretouched authenticity!"

Getting Started

Harrison emphasizes darkroom work for his students. He recommends shooting extensively, taking notes on exposures and apertures, and then working in the darkroom and taking more notes on the results.

"The more photographs you take, the better," Harrison advises photographers starting to develop their professional interests. "The more times you go out and photograph, the more you have to come into the darkroom to develop film, and, consequently, the more comfortable you feel developing film. The more you develop film, the more times you have to print. The more you print, the more comfortable and knowledgeable you will become about printing. It's like riding a bike," says Harrison. "The more you do it, the better you're going to get.

"But you have to want to do it. I can't make you want to do it. I can provide you with the information and technical knowledge and guidance, but the bottom line still is that it has to come from you, the individual. And those are my best students, the ones who are still doing it today because they understood that 'I'm not doing it to please Harrison Branch, I'm doing it because this is what I love to do.'"

Equipment

If you're just starting out, Harrison cautions against spending thousands of dollars on equipment. The payback is very slow, and you may decide that photography is not your bag. You don't want to end up stuck with a lot of sophisticated equipment you're not using. A moderately priced 35 mm camera and a couple of lenses will get you started.

Once you are ready to make a commitment, though, he recommends buying only high-quality equipment, and, if you can afford it, investing in a medium-format camera because of the increased size of the negative.

The Artist's Portfolio

The portfolio is what will get your work out, which is the primary goal of the fine art photographer. It should contain the very best of what you do. It should include work that is representative of what your concerns are as a visual artist. If you work only in black and white, then don't include the two or three color pieces you did five years ago. The portfolio should represent what you are currently involved with as a creative photographer.

Depending on the type of work you do, you might want to include an artist's statement about your work that covers your intent, your motivation, your experiences, or whatever is relevant for the viewer who is looking at your images. Some would argue that text is superfluous, that your photographs must stand on their own merits. This, as with many other elements of fine art, is a debate that you must decide for yourself.

You will also want to include a resume. If you've had previous exhibits, list these according to date and location, as well as whether the work was shown as a solo show or as part of a group exhibit, an invitational or juried exhibit. Also include any educational background or relevant work experience. The gallery director will be interested to know that you taught a workshop on silver gelatin printing but not that you flipped burgers at McDonald's. Most galleries will post a resume of the artist's work during a solo or two- or three-person exhibit, so you will want to have one prepared.

Getting Your Portfolio to the Galleries

Before you can line up a show to get your work seen by the public, you need to have it scrutinized by any number of gallery directors. It isn't essential that you live in the same community in which the gallery operates, but it definitely helps. In New York City, especially, gallery directors like to be able to bring potential clients to your studio or darkroom to meet with you and discuss your work.

Contemporary galleries, especially those in major cities, are most likely going to be interested in your work if it is experimental both in content and in technique. Creative artists are always "pushing the envelope" of the medium, seeking innovative means of expression or presentation that will capture the viewer's eye or imagination. Many galleries, however, are looking for highly traditional or representational images that appeal to a broader audience of clients. These include nature galleries, wildlife galleries, and Western galleries, among others.

Photographer's Market can help provide clues to discover which gallery is appropriate for your work. It lists more than two hundred galleries interested in showing work by photographers. Some of these are museums, others are university art galleries, but most are galleries dedicated to fine art photography. Look for galleries that are interested in the kind of work you do. Don't bother sending beautiful floral color photographs to the Silver Image Gallery, for example. At the same time, sending abstract photos to a gallery that specializes in wildlife and scenics is a waste of postage.

Art in America magazine publishes an annual directory of artists, museums, and galleries. It isn't indexed for photography museums, but you can look through the artist index for people you know to be photographers; then check out the galleries where they are represented. Finding artists whose work is in a similar category with yours is the clue to whether or not the gallery will be an appropriate choice.

Often a gallery will want to represent you without making the commitment for a one-person show. This is a foot in the door. But you will want to bring the gallery new work at least twice a year and make sure your work is actually being shown to prospective clients. If your work can sell from the stacks—the work stacked in racks or flat files at the back of the gallery—you're much more likely to be granted an exhibit.

Other Exhibition Opportunities

Galleries and museums aren't the only places where photography can be shown and offered for sale. Sometimes corporations, restaurants, and other businesses have lobbies or other public areas where they show artists' work. Sometimes these less formal exhibits can be very beneficial for the new artist—you never know who might notice your work during the dessert course or while waiting in the lobby for the elevator. In these situations, the owner of the building or restaurant is not as likely to take a high commission on any sales. Frequently they take no commission at all.

Income Potential

The likelihood of making a living as a fine art photographer is directly proportional to the level of name recognition you enjoy: the better known you are, the more money you'll make. People will know your work, will ask for it in the galleries, and, consequently, galleries will be happy to carry your work because they know it will sell. Your reputation doesn't have to be a national one. If you can develop a strong following in your hometown, you can count on consistent sales and then build on that reputation in surrounding areas.

Galleries take a substantial commission from all sales, generally 40 to 60 percent, so you will want to price your work in such a way that the net amount is acceptable to you. Gallery directors will advise you if they think you've priced yourself out of the market, or, conversely, if they think you've underpriced your work.

Most galleries will want an exclusive relationship with you, at least in the city or area in which the gallery is located. Such relationships are open to negotiation, but having exclusive rights to sell work by particular artists is one means by which galleries establish a clientele.

You will also want to have a separate price for work that has been matted and framed to help compensate you for these additional expenses. Some galleries prefer to frame work themselves to maintain a sense of consistency in the gallery.

The pricing of your work is dependent on the market in which it is being offered for sale, the demand for your work or for your style of photography, and the expense involved in producing the work. Individual photographs can range in price from $50 to $15,000, although the latter would be for a limited-edition print by a well-known photographer whose work is being actively sought by a wide group of collectors.

Grants

A number of public and private foundations provide funding for artists to work on specific projects or to have the freedom for a period of time to pursue their artwork without the need to seek employment unrelated to art. Most states have arts councils that offer individual artist grants, and photography is generally included as one of the eligible art media. Major foundations such as the National Endowment for the Arts and the Guggenheim Foundation also make substantial grants to visual artists.

Related Careers in Fine Art Photography

Art Photographer

As an artist yourself, you understand the importance of visual presentation of artwork, and you have the specialized photography skills that many other fine artists lack. Artists need portfolios in order to present their work to galleries, and the better the photographs, the better the artwork will be represented.

Working independently, you can establish a good business as an art portfolio photographer, particularly if you live in a city with a larger-than-average artist community, such as New York, Los Angeles, San Francisco, Santa Fe, or Seattle. Art galleries also call upon art photographers to take photographs of work by artists they represent.

Staff photographer opportunities are available on museum staffs and auction houses such as Christie's, which has branches in major cities around the world, including New York, London,

Amsterdam, Paris, and Hong Kong. Jerry Markovitz worked for the Metropolitan Museum of Art in New York, where he photographed new acquisitions in the museum's enormous art collection. He was one of five photographers on a media staff of twenty.

A salaried museum photographer might start at $17,000 to $25,000. A freelancer's income is limited only by the number of artist clients, the going rate for art photography work, and how many clients can be scheduled into the year.

Photography Gallery Director

Often the owner of a fine art photography gallery will prefer to turn over the curatorial and daily operations tasks to a gallery director. A fine art gallery director must have an extensive knowledge of both traditional and contemporary photography techniques, the history of photography and photographers, and the current trends in the fine art of photography.

A photographer with enough capital might decide to open a gallery and run it. A photography gallery conducts exhibits of contemporary art, either presenting one or two photographers at a time, or a group exhibit of work by several photographers. Photographs are offered for sale, both from the exhibit walls and from the stacks, usually an extensive collection of photographs kept in archivally controlled flat files or framed and in racks.

Earnings in this volatile field depend on who is responsible for the overhead and, to a large extent, the overall economy. Art is a luxury for most people, and during economic downturns, art sales drop dramatically. Median annual earnings in 2000 were $31,460.

Museum Photography Curator

Several museums in the country have developed extensive photography collections, which are curated—reviewed, selected, and purchased—by a photography curator. A photography curator would need a strong background in the history of photography and fine art photography, either as an art historian or as a fine art photographer with a degree in art history.

Opportunities in this field are limited to large cities or institutional museums or galleries. According to the *Occupational Outlook Handbook*, median annual earnings of curators and museum technicians in 2000 were $33,080. The middle 50 percent earned between $24,740 and $45,490, while the lowest 10 percent earned less than $19,200, and the highest 10 percent earned more than $61,490. Earnings vary considerably by the type and size of the employer, the geographic region, and the specialty. Salaries for curators in large, well-funded museums can be much higher than those in small museums and galleries.

For More Information

Organizations

American Photographic Artisans Guild
P.O. Box 1873
Tacoma, WA 98401
www.apag.net

Association of International Photography Art Dealers
1609 Connecticut Avenue NW
Washington, DC 20009
www.artline.com/associations/ipa/ipa.html

Council on Fine Art Photography
5613 Johnson Avenue
West Bethesda, MD 20817

En Foco, Inc.
32 East Kingsbridge Road
Bronx, NY 10468
www.enfoco.org

International Center of Photography
1114 Avenue of the Americas
New York, NY 10036
www.icp.org

Books and Pamphlets

Photo Gallery & Workshop Handbook, by Jeff Cason. Images Press.
The Keepers of Light: A History and Working Guide to Early Photographic Processes, by William Crawford. Morgan and Morgan.
Successful Fine Art Photography, by Harold Davis. Images Press.
Photography Galleries and Selected Museums: A Survey and International Directory, by Max Lent et al. Max Lent Productions.
The Photographer's Guide to Getting & Having a Successful Exhibition, by Robert S. Persky. Consultant Press.

Periodicals

Aperture
20 East Twenty-Third Street
New York, NY 10010
www.aperture.org
   (Quarterly magazine of fine art and contemporary photography.)

Art Calendar
P.O. Box 2675
Salisbury, MD 21802
www.artcalendar.com
   (Includes gallery listings, grants information, and articles of interest in the fine arts eleven times annually.)

Nueva Luz
32 East Kingsbridge Road
Bronx, NY 10468
www.enfoco.org
   (A triannual journal, featuring fine art by photographers of African, Asian, Latino, and Native American heritage in the United States.)

CHAPTER THIRTEEN

More Careers for Shutterbugs

Related Opportunities in Photography

If you crave cameras and equipment, dig the darkroom, or like to keep things in motion, you've a whole range of career options to choose from. Clicking the shutter is what comes to mind first when we think of photography, but there are many jobs to be done that are essential if photographers are to see their photographs in print.

Working Magic: Darkroom Technicians and Photo Processors

I remember as a child watching my father developing some photographs he'd taken with his old Brownie. We were in a makeshift darkroom he'd created in the downstairs bathroom. The memory of place and time are fuzzy, but I vividly remember the sense of magic as I watched a plain piece of paper, floating in a bath of what looked to my five-year-old eyes like water, transform into an image of my mother and sisters and me at a lake where we'd been camping. I was speechless with the wonder of it.

When I took my first photography class, venturing into a real darkroom with labeled brown bottles and large tubs for the developer and fixer baths, I recaptured that singular delight in the magical appearance of images before my eyes. It's no wonder many who are interested in photography choose careers in the processing and printing of film created by others.

Darkroom Film Processing and Printing

Aside from its inherent fascination, the work of photofinishing and printing is a major industry. Photofinishing sales represented $7.2 billion annually at the end of the 1990s. There are many job opportunities in this field, from one-hour processing labs that require little experience to custom labs that serve professional photographers with high-quality processing and printing.

The overall employment outlook shows little or no change through 2010. The recent increase in digital camera sales have cut into the processing market to a certain degree, but there's been an increase in the number of people who want either to transfer their film images to CD or to obtain photographic prints from their digital cameras. According to the *Occupational Outlook Handbook,* the population increase and the popularity of amateur photography will balance the decline caused by those moving to digital photography. Photographic process workers and machine operators held more than seventy-five thousand jobs in 2000.

Most photo processing workers receive on-the-job training in how to operate the machines and mix the chemicals for developing and printing film. A high school diploma is the minimum requirement, but experience with photography courses in darkroom processing is valuable.

Employees are usually paid by the hour, and rates vary according to the worker's skill and experience, the type of organization, and the geographic region. Median hourly earnings reported in 2000 ranged around $8.00, with drugstores paying the least, at $6.89. Department stores paid a median of $7.97, and custom labs paid the highest rate, at $9.03 per hour.

Another survey showed photofinishing technicians earning a median base salary of $17,165. Photographic processing machine operators earned a median annual salary of $25,565, with a low of $21,198 and a high of $31,920. Employees in this position often needed a two-year associate's degree or equivalent experience.

Advancement into management positions requires additional specialized training in photography and photo processing mechanics or in the machinery used in the processing and printing of film. Supervisors, assistant managers, managers, and department heads are all positions of responsibility that can be achieved by starting as an unskilled film processing technician.

Custom Photo Labs

The most specialized of photography labs are those serving the needs of professional photographers and portrait studios. The demand for quality is high and standards are exacting. These labs process most of the work by hand, taking individual care with each job, rather than using color processing machines found at large commercial labs or one-hour labs.

Other custom labs exist in corporate or industrial situations, most especially at camera and film manufacturing plants. Some large portrait or commercial photography studios incorporate their own custom labs on-site, and most large newspaper and magazine publishers operate on-site darkrooms with specially hired darkroom technicians rather than photographers processing film. Some universities, too, have on-campus darkroom operations that serve public relations needs, as well as photo work for academic departments.

Employment in these labs requires a high level of skill, experience, and training beyond basic darkroom photography. You must have thorough knowledge of film and its properties and the chemistry involved in its development and printing and the ability to control these variables to produce prints and transparencies that do justice to the professional photographer's vision. A good custom lab technician forms a partnership with the photographer to produce the best possible results.

One-Hour Photo Labs

These photo processing minilabs are popping up all over the country. In my small town, there are at least six places where I can drop off film and come back in an hour or a few days for my prints. One place even offers drive-through film processing and espresso! About one-fourth of all photofinishing workers are employed in these labs. The processing machines require very little technical skill to operate. Because the machines process and print an undeveloped roll of color film in only two size options, enlargements and reprints are still sent out to commercial labs.

Depending on the size of the lab, opportunities for advancement might include assistant manager or manager positions. Salaries at this level range from $12 to $15 per hour or $24,000 to $30,000 per year. With experience in this field, advancement into commercial or custom lab management is a natural step.

Commercial Photo Labs

These large processing plants represent about 25 percent of all photographic processing employment opportunities. They serve drugstores, grocery stores, and other retail outlets that offer drop-off services for photo finishing. They also provide enlargement and reprint services that the one-hour machines don't handle.

Commercial processing labs also serve the large amateur photography market. The equipment used to develop and print film is extremely sophisticated, so the workers do not need to be highly skilled in photographic processing to operate them. Still, opportunities exist here for skilled developers, who are hired in supervisory or management positions.

In commercial labs, the print developers attach the film from a film canister to a leader on the machine, attach sensitized paper for printing, and then, while operating the machine, check it for temperature controls and watch as the prints emerge to make sure the prints are being processed accurately. Any problems are referred to the quality control supervisor.

In addition to processing film for prints, commercial labs handle reprints, enlargements, cropping, and special printing requirements. These tasks are handled by individuals with experience in developing and darkroom technology.

Courses in photography, darkroom processing, chemistry, and mathematics can be beneficial in photofinishing. Most photo processing workers in commercial labs have at least a high school diploma, while many hold two-year certification from community or vocational colleges or technical institutes. Certification can enhance opportunities for supervisory or management positions. On-the-job training programs provide advancement opportunities and specialization, which can lead to self-employment or employment with custom labs. Many of the larger photo processing labs offer continuing education training to keep employees on top of emerging technologies.

The Digital Technology Boom

According to *Specialty Lab Update*, a newsletter published for commercial labs and in-house photo finishing labs, "commercial labs have aggressively embraced electronic imaging services," while people labs, those primarily serving professional photographers and portrait studios, "have taken a wait-and-see approach."

The most popular applications of electronic imaging thus far, according to Ted Fox, Photo Marketing Association Group Executive for Marketing Information, are computer-generated slides for presentations, desktop publishing, electronic photo composition, and photo retouching and restoration.

Kathy Polce is a lab manager for Picture Magician in Rochester, New York, a photo specialty store that focuses entirely on digital finishing, products, and services. She operates three Picture Preview centers that allow patrons to drop off film for processing to CD, then when they return they can preview and select the images they want, zoom in or crop to improve composition, and order multiple prints of a single image or any combination of quantities for images on a roll of film. According to Kathy, the preview-and-select option "gives customers more control of their pictures, and we made a commitment to educate the staff so they could talk knowledgeably with customers and explain all the features and advantages."

The increasing popularity of electronic imaging in commercial labs opens the door for employment in higher-skilled and, therefore, higher-wage positions. Experience with photo software such as Photoshop is a benefit. Marketing of these new services has been challenging for many commercial companies, so if you present good ideas for bringing in new customers, you'll have excellent job prospects.

Photo Retouching and Restoration

When I was in high school and had been elected the head of an organization I belonged to, my new position required that I get a professional portrait done. I was devastated to wake up on the morning of the photo session and discover not one but three blemishes. The heartbreak of teen-age acne!

"Not to worry!" said the photographer. "I'll just have the photo retouched and you won't notice a thing." More darkroom magic. The end result was wonderful. I looked much better in that photograph than I ever did in the mirror! It's still one of my favorites.

Photographic retouch artists work with air brushes, tiny paint brushes with specially blended chemicals and pigments, and/or computer programs to remove spots from negatives, smooth skin tones in portraits, blend out objects in the background, and generally enhance the image. Photo restoration involves copying a photograph that has been damaged or is deteriorating, then retouching the negative to try to rebuild or re-create the missing portions of the original.

Training in photographic retouching and restoration can happen in college courses, specialized training seminars, and on the job with custom photography labs. Employment opportunities exist in custom labs, professional portrait and commercial studios, large commercial labs, and industrial or corporate in-house facilities. Major chain operations frequently offer restoration work, which is sent to centralized processing labs with retouch and restoration artists on staff.

A skilled photo retoucher can also find employment as an independent, establishing a relationship with a number of processing labs and professional photographers. The earning potential for a professional retouch artist can be between $30 and $75 per hour.

Camera Sales

All those photographers, both the professionals and the millions of hobbyists, bought their cameras somewhere. There are thousands of retail outlets, several major mail-order companies, and hundreds of Internet outlets, plus a number of opportunities for selling cameras wholesale. All offer job opportunities for camera enthusiasts.

What You Need to Know

Whether you work in a retail store, the camera section of a large department store, or as a representative for one of the many camera manufacturing companies, selling cameras requires a thorough knowledge both of the merchandise and of photography itself. You need to be able to respond to questions about how the camera performs under various conditions, and you need to be responsive to questions or complaints from your customers.

One of the most basic requirements for any job in the retail sales business is an interest in people. If you enjoy working with a wide variety of people and like to answer questions and swap stories about photography and cameras, camera sales is a career path that you might enjoy.

Corporate Sales Representative

A camera sales or marketing representative working for Nikon or Olympus or Minolta or any of the other camera producers is assigned a territory to cover. The representative is more than a salesperson who travels to retail camera stores in the assigned territory to sell camera equipment. This person also serves as a resource of information about the cameras and the company's customer support. Larger camera stores often hold seminars for customers interested in a particular line of cameras, and the representative might be asked to lead the seminar or be on hand to answer questions. The representative also trains the retail salespeople so that they will be able to explain to their customers the special features of the equipment.

In addition to direct selling skills, a knowledge of marketing and advertising strategies is also helpful. Toward this end, it is often helpful to have a degree or course work in business or marketing to complement your knowledge of photography and cameras. The sales representative often assists the retail stores in developing advertisements for the products. Sales records for each store must be analyzed to be certain that the right products are being offered for sale based on the store owner's knowledge of store patrons and the sales representative's analysis of previous trends.

Other sales opportunities include trade show or mail-order representatives. The territorial sales representative may also handle trade shows, and mail-order sales representatives might work for a separate branch of a large photographic retailer.

Photographic equipment was one of the leading commodities imported in the United States, representing $5.6 billion in 2000, according to the Foreign Trade Division of the Department of Commerce. Each of the leading camera manufacturing companies—Kodak, Canon, Nikon, Olympus, Minolta, Pentax—employs an extensive sales force throughout the United States and Canada.

Sales representatives generally receive a base salary, plus commissions and reimbursement for expenses. Companies might also offer incentives or bonuses for the sale of higher-priced items. Sales representatives can expect to earn between $21,450 and $57,280, depending on their sales success.

Retail Sales

Virtually every town with a population of twenty thousand or more has some store where you can buy a camera, whether it's the back counter at the local department store, the camera department at Wal-Mart, or the Nikon counter at New York's famous Willoughby's. While the pay is not as significant in retail sales for camera or department stores, working in camera sales can provide an excellent opportunity to learn about cameras and their manufacturers as you develop your career in photography.

Retail sales clerks can expect a starting hourly wage equivalent to minimum wage or slightly higher. You'll be expected to absorb a tremendous amount of information on the job about the cameras, both new and used, being offered for sale, as well as the film and its processing. With the expansion of your knowledge and responsibilities, you could earn between $10.54 and $15.86 per hour, plus commission.

Dan Wilson worked for a large photo retail store in Seattle while studying photography at the University of Washington. He worked part-time while in school and full-time during breaks.

His initial task involved soaking up information from more experienced sales clerks and manufacturer's representatives, helping customers look at used equipment, and selling film. Once he'd developed a strong knowledge base, he began actively selling cameras. For each camera he sold, he received a bonus, or "sales spiff," which varied in amount depending on the value of the camera.

"The salary was never anything to write home about," Dan says, "but I learned so much about cameras and film that I feel it was just an integral part of the education I paid to receive."

Another benefit of the job, according to Dan, was being able to purchase his own camera equipment at a significant discount.

Photographic Equipment Buyer

Photo equipment buyers, on the other hand, command a salary that makes this an attractive career choice. Buyers are employed by the larger department stores and camera stores and may have responsibility for attending trade shows and sales seminars offered by the equipment manufacturers. A degree in business or marketing is a definite plus in this position, but along with this must come experience with and a love for photography, cameras, and equipment.

The buyer must be able to look at sales trends and keep track of developments in the photographic equipment industry. A knowledge of the clientele, whether hobbyists or professionals or a mix of skilled amateurs and pro shooters, helps the buyer to determine what should be kept on the store's shelves.

Median annual earnings for retail buyers in 2000 were $33,730, with an average range between $21,570 and $51,560. Earnings increase with additional responsibilities for management.

Retail Sales Manager

The manager in a photography retail store or department has responsibility for training, hiring, scheduling, and analyzing sales and marketing trends. The manager might share responsibility for buying as well as sales on the floor of the department or store.

Middle managers, those with on-site responsibilities for sales and customer support questions, can expect to earn a median salary of $27,510 annually. Salaries vary according to the size of the company and the geographic region. In 2000, salaries averaged between $21,050 and $37,200 for retail sales managers, according to the *Occupational Outlook Handbook*. Middle managers usually rise from the ranks of experienced retail sales clerks. District or regional managers for larger chain operations earn up to $68,520.

Camera Repair

Camera repair is closely related to retail sales because camera stores often service and repair the cameras they sell, either on-site or as a clearinghouse for the various manufacturers they represent. If you're interested in the intricate workings of the camera's interior, a career in camera repair can provide challenges for years. The new developments in cameras each year mean the technician must keep up to date with the changes, as well as maintain a working knowledge of older cameras that are still in use.

Jeff Owen runs his own camera repair shop in Ontario, California. He'd been interested in photography in high school, and after a knee injury forced him to leave his job in construction work, he started selling cameras in a small town camera store. He was active in photography as a hobby, so the job suited him.

"The store, like most, had several junk cameras that customers had brought in but had refused the repair estimates and never returned to claim," Jeff recalls. "I'd always been pretty good at fixing things, so I decided to take some apart and see what made them tick. I found I was able to figure out the mechanics and managed to get some of them working. I then found a nice repair guy in Los Angeles who was willing to answer my questions and get me started in repair."

Jeff also studied electronics and read all he could about the mechanics and electronics of cameras. "I then started going to training seminars and still do in order to stay on top of the new technology. I will buy a camera once I see that it is going to be a reasonably frequent repair job, then take it apart to learn how to fix it on my own before I try to do that to a customer's camera."

Jeff now works as an independent contractor. "It's not easy to get into this business, but there are a few ways of learning the trade," Jeff explains. "Most techs end up getting jobs with manufacturers and learning their cameras, then going to work for independent repair shops specializing in whatever they did at the factory. Others, like myself, who can fix a wide variety of manufacturers' equipment, just keep hitting the books and learning new cameras as they come out."

Vocational technical schools, community colleges, home study courses, manufacturing associations, and the Society of Photo-Technicians offer opportunities for training in this field.

Job Options and Earnings

Technicians are hired by large retail stores, manufacturers, and specialty repair shops. Whether you're paid an hourly wage or by the repair project, earnings range from $12,000 per year for a trainee to a median of $27,920 per year, or $13.94 per hour, as a technician. Advancement within manufacturing company repair departments to management with supervisory responsibilities brings pay levels to between $30,835 and $36,598.

The specialized skills of the camera repair technician make it possible for you to work on your own, establishing client relationships with retail owners in your area, as well as individual camera owners. Your hours are your own, and the earning potential equals or perhaps exceeds—depending on how much work you take in and the prevailing rates for repair work in your area—what you might make as an employee for someone else.

Teaching

The teaching of photography is an extensive profession that encompasses virtually every college, university, community college, and high school in the country, not to mention special vocational schools, adult education programs, and the many thousands of workshops and seminars offered throughout the United States and Canada.

For most teachers, this is a full-time career choice. For others, particularly those offering seminars or workshops, teaching is a means of giving to others the benefit of their own education, skills, and experience.

While teaching has the advantages of long vacations, good benefits, and a livable salary, teachers earn every one of those benefits. Keeping the interest and attention of—not to mention inspiring and genuinely teaching—a roomful of fifteen- to eighteen-year-olds in high school, or eighteen- to twenty-one-year-olds in college, takes a great deal of planning and patience. It also takes its toll both physically and emotionally.

Teaching Photography in High Schools

The curriculum in public high school programs varies from state to state, from district to district. Whether the school offers courses in photography often depends on the school's budget. If there's room for electives, photography is one of the most popular.

The photography teacher might come to teaching through an art background or through a degree in photojournalism. In every state, public high school teachers must have at least a bachelor's degree and certification or a license for teaching. Some states require that teachers earn a master's degree during the first ten years of teaching. Private schools are not bound by the certification requirements, but most require a college degree.

The high school photography curriculum is basic and general, providing students with an understanding of taking photographs, using the camera, and processing and printing in the darkroom. The photography teacher also might be responsible for supervising the student newspaper and yearbook staffs or for teaching other subject areas, such as art or journalism.

Salaries for high school teachers vary from state to state, but the national median per ten-month school year ranged from $37,610 to $42,080 in 2000, according to the *Occupational Outlook Handbook*. The top of the pay scale for teachers was between $57,590 and $64,920, more if they teach summer school.

Teaching Photography in Colleges

Photography professors on college and university campuses are generally found in either the fine art department or in the department of journalism. Depending on the size of the photography program, there may be only one photographer or as many as twenty at a school such as the Rochester Institute of Technology in New York or Brooks Institute of Photography in California, which are considered by many to be the most comprehensive photography programs in the country.

More than three hundred colleges and universities offer degrees in photography, while photography courses are offered at nearly all others. The number of courses taught by college faculty varies according to the size of the institution and whether faculty are required to pursue professional research or, in the case of photographers, exhibition or publication. At a teaching-oriented institution, faculty might teach three to four courses per quarter or semester. At research institutions, the teaching load might vary from one to four courses per term.

To teach at the college level, you need a "terminal degree," which for photographers most likely means a master of fine arts degree (M.F.A.). For photojournalists, the equivalent might be a master's degree in photojournalism or an M.F.A. in photography. Generally, only professors of the history of photography would pursue a Ph.D.

The median annual salary for college teachers was $46,330 in 2000, according to the *Occupational Outlook Handbook*. The middle 50 percent earned between $32,270 and $66,460. The lowest 10 percent earned less than $21,700, and the highest 10 percent earned more than $87,850. Salaries at public colleges tend to be lower than those at private universities but higher than two-year institutions.

Teaching Photography in Vocational-Technical Schools and Community Colleges

Teaching photography in vocational-technical, community or junior college, or adult education programs often takes a very specific, job-oriented approach. The curriculum focuses on the basic issues of learning to use the camera effectively, understanding darkroom techniques, and mastering the essentials of lighting and composition. Although the photography courses at junior colleges might be taught in the art department, the main emphasis will be on the practical aspects of photography rather than more advanced creative exploration.

To teach at this level, you must have a bachelor's degree or, increasingly, a master's degree. Some states might require additional credentials for teaching at public institutions. Salary levels are slightly lower at community colleges and two-year institutions than those at colleges and universities.

Teaching Photography Workshops for Aspiring Professionals

Photography workshops are offered on a wide range of topics, including ambient light, zone system photographic techniques, infrared, still life, wildlife, glamour, fashion, and virtually any subject in front of or behind the camera lens. You'll find workshops on marketing your photographs, getting your work exhibited in art galleries, and finding your own personal "vision."

Photographers who lead workshops and seminars are typically working professionals with a great deal of experience in a specific area of photography. There are a number of established workshop programs or institutes that offer short-course seminars throughout the year. Some workshops are only offered during summer months or off-season times for the university professors or professional photographers who teach them.

The annual *Photographer's Market* lists more than two hundred established workshops, and several photography magazines include listings regularly, either as part of a regular feature or in the classified ad section.

Individual tuition fees for these seminars range from $35 per day to $21,000 for a ten-month residential program. The costs cover all expenses and overhead, including the instructor's fee. Experienced individuals who establish their own seminars, therefore, have tremendous earning potential, but one must factor in the expenses of advertising and facilities.

Teaching Basic Courses for Photo Buffs

In addition to the professional workshop circuit, many local organizations offer basic photography courses for hobbyists. Depending on the organization, the fee charged, and the number of students you can handle at a given session, this can provide a worthwhile sideline to a freelance career. It's also just plain fun helping to turn someone else on to the enjoyment of photography.

Photographer's Representative

Many photographers, especially those whose work is in demand, don't have time to take care of the business end of photography—promoting themselves to potential clients, arranging meetings, scheduling photo sessions, and negotiating fees. They'd much rather be behind the camera than on the phone or behind a desk. That's where the photographer's representative comes in. The rep works much like a literary agent. It's the rep's job to match the photographer with the clients, make the contacts, and sell the photographer as the best one to be hired for a particular project—or for future projects. The rep also handles contract negotiations, which, although a time-consuming and tedious process, determines both the photographer's and the representative's incomes.

Photographer's representatives work for several photographers at once but will usually seek to present one specific photographer for a given job or client, working to match the photographer's style and specialization with the client's needs. Reps make sales presentations to art directors and department heads of major corporations and advertising agencies. They need strong sales skills, as well as good organizational and negotiating skills.

Representatives may work with a consortium of representatives, both literary agents and artist's representatives, or alone. Photo reps work in major metropolitan areas, primarily New York, Los Angeles, and Chicago. Earnings are based on a percentage of the negotiated fee for the photographer, so the more work and better pay you can gain for your photographers, the more you earn.

Motion Pictures: Film, Video, Television

The moving pictures industry—whether the Hollywood movie machine, the local television news, or wedding videography—provides enough opportunities for an entire book by itself. This book, therefore, will only present a brief introduction to some of the opportunities in movie and video as an acknowledgment of the close relationship between moving and still photography.

In virtually any area of photography discussed elsewhere in this book, you will find a market for moving images, as well as for still photography. Even magazines are starting to come out on CD-ROM and incorporate video or movie clips as part of the overall package. The future of video technology is changing all the time.

Motion Pictures

The movie industry is almost exclusively operated in the rarefied world of Hollywood, a part of the sprawling landscape that is collectively known as Los Angeles. Some film work is done in New York and Miami, but the majority is done in Los Angeles or, when on location elsewhere in the world, by film crews based in L.A.

Los Angeles is also home to two major universities offering degree programs in cinematography: the University of California at Los Angeles (UCLA) and the University of Southern California (USC). A degree in cinematography is no guarantee of a job. For that you need talent, reliability, good contacts, and a lot of luck.

The ultimate goal of many a camera operator is to be a film director. Others are quite happy with the title director of photography, which is one of the categories for the annual Oscar awards. The movie business offers a broad range of challenges, as well as the potential for a lucrative career.

Camera Operators. Any aspect of the movie industry is difficult to break into, whether you're an aspiring actor or a would-be camera operator. The reality is that there are far more people eager to do the jobs than there are jobs to be done. It's a glamorous industry, suffused with excitement and the promise of a big payoff—someday. Getting started means sweeping floors, running errands, moving props, and anything else that gets you "on the set." From there, making connections, showing your film clips to anyone who will look at them, and just plain luck are what might open the right doors. The entry-level position in this business is film loader; then you progress to second assistant camera operator, first assistant, then camera operator. Most camera workers in the motion picture business belong to the International Cinematographers Guild or the Society of Operating Cameramen.

According to the *Occupational Outlook Handbook,* median annual earnings for camera operators were $27,870 in 2000, with a low of less than $14,130 and a high of more than $63,690. The middle 50 percent earned between $19,230 and $44,150.

Special Effects and Animation. Harley Jessup works for Industrial Light and Magic, the company that brought us the special effects in *ET* as well as *Star Wars, Hook,* and a number of films requiring a little industrial magic. His training is as a graphic designer, but a great deal of his work involves photography, including movie film, still photography, and frame-by-frame motion pictures. Will Vinton, creator of the California Raisins, works on a frame-by-frame basis to animate the claymation figures of his now famous commercials. A full-length feature film, *Chicken Run,* was made using this technology. Computer animation has become a major industry in the last decade, with films such as *Toy Story* and *A Bug's Life* making movie news.

Camera operators in special effects and animation can earn from a modest $24,800 per year for a small studio to $70,000 or more per year at a larger organization involved with big-budget pictures. Creativity, an artist's eye, and a technician's capabilities are all prerequisites in this exciting new field.

Television

According to Nielsen Media Research, the company that brings us the Nielsen Ratings of television programs, 98 percent of Americans own a color television set, and the average American household has the set turned on for about seven hours every day.

Each program on television involves camera operators or, as they're sometimes called, engineers. Comedies, mysteries, dramas, made-for-television movies, and news programs are filmed by camera operators who belong to either the International Alliance of Theater and State Employees or the National Association of Broadcast Employees and Technicians. The majority of television programs are filmed in New York or Los Angeles. Some are also shot on location. Beginners should look for jobs at one of the many smaller local stations throughout the country or at a cable television network.

Television Advertising. Major advertising agencies rather than television networks or stations are the employers of advertising filmmakers. The making of an advertisement is not unlike the making of a television program or motion picture. There's a director, an art director, a producer (the client), a camera operator, and a host of behind-the-scenes stylists and assistants. The pay scale for camera operators in this demanding industry, as with the advertising industry for still photographers, is significantly higher than for many other areas.

Corporate and Industrial Film Work

The needs for videos and films in the corporate and industrial world are many and varied. Companies, organizations, and governmental agencies all hire camera operators and filmmakers to create nontheatrical films with a specific message and purpose. Large corporations have camera operators on staff but might also hire independents. The starting position in corporate film work is production assistant.

Here are a few of the uses for film and video work in business and industry:

- Training films
- Product advertising and marketing videos
- Headhunter videos designed to attract top executives to work for large corporations
- Informational videos that promote products, an organization or company, or operations or procedures
- Sales videos that provide the sales representatives with information about products and sales strategies
- New purchaser videos that give instructions to consumers on how to use or apply products they've purchased

Freelance Videography

One of the drawbacks to working on your own in the film industry is the expense of both equipment and film—not to mention processing. The relatively inexpensive video recorders and camcorders, which use video cassettes, and digital camcorders that download directly to computers have made motion picture photography accessible in the way the first inexpensive cameras brought still photography to the masses. With proper training, experience, and that intangible "photographer's eye," you can become a valuable asset to a variety of potential clients.

Aside from a camcorder or video recorder, you need to have some means of editing the movies you make. Unless all you are doing is creating an inventory of objects for insurance purposes, you will need to rearrange the visual information you've recorded. It's impossible to imagine being able to plan so carefully and film so perfectly that all elements of a video appear in proper sequence without any extraneous details.

The computer has made video editing more simple and less expensive. With a minimal investment in equipment—a digital camcorder with cables to both VCR and computer, and the necessary software—you're ready to roll. New Macintosh computers come loaded with an easy-to-use and fairly powerful editing program called iMovie as well as iDVD, a program that records, or burns, DVDs. Here are some examples of the kind of work you can find as a freelance videographer:

- Real estate videos showing properties available for sale
- Art videos for exhibition in modern galleries
- Sports videos for children's sports events, local team sports, or collegiate sports
- Children's dance recitals or school programs
- Horse or pet show videos for sales to individual
- Personal music videos for aspiring musicians
- Audition videos for aspiring actors
- Videotapes of meetings for organizations, public hearings for government agencies, or presentations for businesses
- Training tapes for business and industry
- Demonstration tapes on products and services
- Self-critique tapes for professionals in all areas who want to "see" how they're doing their jobs
- How-to videos for mail-order marketing
- Witness interviews for legal cases
- Videotaped resumes or job applications and interviews

Photography Writer

One final career option is the photographer who combines a deep knowledge of the medium with a desire to inform others about the industry. The photography writer does all kinds of writing about photography: equipment reviews, informational articles, editorials or opinion pieces, and magazine articles on every conceivable subject related to photography.

These writers work for camera, film, and photography equipment manufacturers, marketing companies, and magazines or trade publications. They might also work as freelancers, combining photography experience and writing skills to sell articles to a variety of clients. They are also book authors, writing about photographic methods, techniques, and genres to help photographers learn more about the craft.

A salaried writer earns between $18,000 and $43,000 per year, depending on the employer. A writer with responsibility for advertising copy earns a bit more than one who works strictly on editorial text. Freelance photography writers earn their incomes through magazine sales, primarily, or from book royalties.

Some Final Words of Advice from Someone Who's Done It All

Andy Baird started photographing with box Brownies as a child. He progressed through early Polaroids to a 35 mm Argus in his teens. He stumbled into a science photography career out of high school, traveled to Costa Rica on a research project funded by the National Geographic Society, built his own processing drum for his kitchen "darkroom," built a microcomputer, and wrote his own paint programs. He got involved with computers when the first PCs hit the market, and he explored their potential for enhancing photography. He started making multimedia CDs before most people knew that CD didn't always mean "certificate of deposit." Throughout all these experiences, photography has been a mainstay. Andy offers some sage advice with which to end this book.

- **Start simple.** Learn the basics of photography before you invest in that auto-everything SLR. A few months or years spent with an all-manual camera will give you a solid foundation to build on. Start with black and white and learn to develop and print—even if, like me, you're drawn to color. Most of all, learn to see. No amount of equipment can help you if you can't do that.

- **Stay simple.** Don't succumb to the old "if only I had this lens, I could take really good/creative/professional photos" syndrome. Over the years I've accumulated a set of lenses ranging from 7.5 mm up to 400 mm, and you know what? I do 95 percent of my shooting with just two lenses: a 24 mm wide angle and a 100 mm macro. Your own favorites may be different, but the point remains: the love of equipment is a snare and a delusion that will lead you astray and fritter away your time and money. Get good equipment, but only get what you really can use—and then use it, abuse it, master it completely before moving on to another purchase.

- **The best accessory is film.** If you're looking for something to spend money on, spend it on film. Never scrimp on film. Keep plenty of it around (your refrigerator's vegetable bin is a good place to stash a few dozen rolls). Don't be afraid to waste it on grab shots, long shots, or other 'risky' pictures. Your mistakes are your best teachers, so be sure to make plenty of mistakes. Take risks, and you'll improve far faster than the careful planner who makes every shot count.

- **Carry a camera everywhere.** Don't think that you can occasionally strap on a camera and go looking for pictures when the mood strikes you—you'll find they elude you. Carry a camera everywhere, all the time, and pictures will seek you out. Even if it's just a point-and-shoot cheapie, having a camera on you at all times does more than ensure you can get those unexpected grab shots. It magically educates your eyes; the mere consciousness of having a camera on your person makes you see better—all the time.

- **Give yourself assignments.** It doesn't matter whether you have a client or a teacher telling you what to photograph. Tell yourself. Assign a subject and then photograph it. Pick something you're interested in—reflections, children, hubcaps, old people—and really study it. Even better, pick something you're not interested in, something mundane, and see whether you can make it interesting by seeing it in a different way.

- **Take notes.** Carry a pocket notebook with your camera, and whenever you can, write down your lighting, exposure, aperture and other variables. The more information you have when you look at the processed images about what you were doing when you took the photo, the better your chance of recreating that serendipitous accident—or avoiding that fatal mistake.

For More Information

Organizations

International Imaging Industry Association
550 Mamaroneck Avenue
Harrison, NY 10528
www.i3a.org

Photo Marketing Association International
3000 Picture Place
Jackson, MI 49201
www.pmai.org

Society of Motion Picture and Television Engineers
595 West Hartsdale Avenue
White Plains, NY 10607
www.smpte.org

Society of Photo-Technologists
11112 Spotted Road
Cheney, WA 99004
www.s-p-t.org

International Cinematographers Guild
7715 Sunset Boulevard, Suite 300
Hollywood, CA 90046
www.cameraguild.com

American Society of Cinematographers
P.O. Box 2230
Hollywood, CA 90078
www.cinematographer.com

Society of Operating Cameramen
P.O. Box 2006
Toluca Lake, CA 91610
www.soc.org

Books

Cash in on Your Camcorder: One Hundred and Two Ways to Make Money with Your Video Camera, by Eileen Stanton. Sandia Publishing.

Periodicals

Photo Lab Management
PLM Publishing
P.O. Box 1703
Santa Monica, CA 90406

Photographic Processing
Cygnus Publishing
445 Broad Hollow Road, Suite 21
Melville, NY 11747

About the Author

C heryl McLean has been a writer, editor, and sometime photographer for nearly twenty years. She owns and operates a desktop publishing, design, editing, and writing business, ImPrint Services, in Corvallis, Oregon. She holds a bachelor's degree in English and a master's in journalism. She taught journalism and writing courses at Western Oregon University and the University of Oregon.

She studied photography independently, and her photographs have been published in books and magazines. Her book, *Oregon's Quiet Waters: A Guide to Lakes for Canoeists and Other Paddlers,* is in its second edition and contains many photographs that help her escape to mountain lakes in her imagination when the workload won't let her get away from the computer.

She has served as president of the board of directors of CALYX, Inc., and on the editorial boards for CALYX Books and *CALYX: A Journal of Art and Literature by Women* since 1979. She handles design and production for CALYX, which has won a variety of national and regional awards for its publications.